Dyslexia and Mathematics
2nd edition

Reviews of the first edition:

'*This book . . . makes excellent reading for anyone involved in the teaching of mathematics.*' **Mathematics in School**.

'. . . a source of valuable practical advice to many practising teachers.' **School Psychology International**.

'*This is an important book in the field of dyslexia.*' **Education**.

In this revised and fully updated 2nd edition of a classic, best-selling text, a formidable team of expert contributors draw on their extensive experience to provide a wealth of material based on individual case studies and research evidence, and supported by practical and accessible teaching strategies.

The new material includes: discussion of the latest thinking in the field (for instance ideas on dyscalculia), information from a survey of primary school children, guidance on suitable testing material, and innovative contributions on practice.

Dyslexia and Mathematics, 2nd edition, is unique in terms of its coverage and authority, and should be a must-buy text for teachers, student teachers, and special needs coordinators.

T.R. Miles, OBE, is Emeritus Professor at the School of Psychology, University of Wales, Bangor.

Elaine Miles is a Consultant at the Dyslexia Unit, University of Wales, Bangor.

Dyslexia and Mathematics
2nd edition

Edited by
T.R. Miles and Elaine Miles

RoutledgeFalmer
Taylor & Francis Group

LONDON AND NEW YORK

First published 2004
by RoutledgeFalmer
11 New Fetter Lane, London EC4P 4EE

Simultaneously published in the USA and Canada
by RoutledgeFalmer
29 West 35th Street, New York, NY 10001

RoutledgeFalmer is an imprint of the Taylor & Francis Group

Typeset in Garamond by
Newgen Imaging Systems (P) Ltd, Chennai, India
Printed and bound in Great Britain by
TJ International Ltd, Padstow, Cornwall

British Library Cataloguing in Publication Data
A catalogue record for this book is available from the British Library

Library of Congress Cataloging in Publication Data
A catalog record for this book has been requested

ISBN 0–415–31817–3 (pbk)
ISBN 0–415–31816–5 (hbk)

Contents

Figures and tables

Contributors

J.R. Ashcroft (B.Ed.) is a former headmaster of Mark College, Somerset.

S.J. Chinn (BSc, PhD) is Principal of Mark College, Somerset.

Ann Dowker (BA, PhD) is a University Research Lecturer in the Department of Experimental Psychology, University of Oxford.

Anne Henderson (B.Ed.) is a former teacher at the Dyslexia Unit, University of Wales, Bangor, and at St. David's College, Llandudno.

Mary Kibel (BA, M.Ed., PGCE, PhD) taught dyslexic pupils at primary and secondary schools in Devon; she also ran workshops for the Devon Dyslexia Association.

Elaine Miles (MA, Dip.Ed.) was Director of Teaching at the Dyslexia Unit, University of Wales, Bangor, and now acts as Dyslexia Consultant.

T.R. Miles (OBE, MA, PhD, C.Psychol., FBPsS) is Professor Emeritus of Psychology at the University of Wales, Bangor.

S.A. Turner Ellis (BA, PhD, PGCE, Dip. Sp. L.D, AMDBA, C.Psychol.) has many years of experience as a Special Needs teacher in Surrey and as a school SENCO in Berkshire.

Preface to the 2nd edition

In the eleven years since the first edition of this book, our knowledge of the difficulties in mathematics experienced by dyslexics has grown considerably. T.R. Miles has discussed some of this evidence in the first chapter. Chinn and Ashcroft have also published a large amount of fresh material on the needs of dyslexic children at the secondary school stage (especially Chinn and Ashcroft 1998), and more recently Dorian Yeo (Yeo 2003) has contributed a book on her experience with children aged $6\frac{1}{2}$ to 9 years, both dyslexic and dyspraxic. This last very recent material has far-reaching implications, and requires further detailed study. The *Numeracy Strategy* (DfEE 1999) has also been published, and this has influenced current thinking on methods of teaching mathematics to the youngest children. At the end of this book a list of *Suggestions for Further Reading* gives details of all these, and also of some of the other relevant publications that have appeared.

We believe, however, that the basic idea which underlay the first edition of this book – that of covering a series of distinct *themes* – still has much to offer. Mary Kibel's imaginative chapter, 'Linking Language to Action' is still as valid as ever; 'Reading and Writing in Mathematics' (Elaine Miles) is important for unravelling the complex issues involved there, while Anne Henderson's wise words press home the need for a listening relationship with the dyslexic pupil, and also for studying the methods that they have found easy up to now, rather than imposing traditional algorithms unilaterally. Finally, as T.R. Miles explains in Chapter 6, structured materials can still play a valuable role for the older pupil and can explain more advanced work – they need not necessarily be childish. These four chapters along with Chapter 7, by Chinn and Ashcroft have required only minimal updating and occasional clarification. The first chapter, and Chapter 2 (Chinn), however, have been substantially rewritten.

We are fortunate to have two new contributors. As a result of research she has done, S.A. Turner Ellis has come to conclusions helpful to teachers with regard to teaching number facts – a very difficult area for dyslexics. Ann Dowker is a lecturer at Oxford University. Ann comes with a refreshing new perspective: she has studied the findings on mathematical handicaps in brain damage cases, and also the abilities in different areas of mathematics to be found in children in the general population, and the different skills involved.

As we made clear in the first edition, it was never our purpose to produce a book on the teaching of mathematics in general. Our central aim was to make some contribution towards the teaching of mathematics to dyslexics. If pupils who have other needs benefit from the suggestions in the book, as some reviewers of the first edition have suggested, this is a bonus.

T.R.M

E.M

Bangor, October 2003

Books mentioned in the Preface are listed in 'Suggested reading' at the end of the book.

Conventions

To avoid ugly circumlocutions, we refer, unless there is good reason otherwise, to the teacher as 'she' and to the pupil as 'he'; we take it as obvious that both teachers and pupils can be of either gender! Similarly, some of the contributors use the word 'dyslexic' as a noun ('a dyslexic'), since this saves having to make cumbersome references to 'dyslexic persons', 'dyslexic individuals', 'people with dyslexia', etc. Dyslexics are people first and foremost, as the contributors to this book are, of course, fully aware – how could anyone doubt it?

Chapter 1

Theoretical background

T.R. Miles

THE NATURE OF DYSLEXIA

Although the manifestations of dyslexia were identified more than a hundred years ago, it is only in the last few decades that there has been recognition of the condition on any large scale. It is perhaps helpful to think of dyslexia as a family of manifestations: these may vary from one individual to another, but in all cases there is an identifiable pattern, and it is this pattern which, despite the differences between individuals, justifies the use of the same diagnostic label, 'dyslexic'.

As far as the acquisition of literacy skills is concerned, there can be no denying that dyslexia is a handicap. Most dyslexics are late in learning to read and have considerable difficulty in learning to spell. The spell check, though useful, is not an infallible guide – for instance it will not correct 'peace' into piece nor 'never the less' into *nevertheless*. Much can be achieved by appropriate tuition, but the problems do not totally disappear. In particular most dyslexics remain slow readers, and although some speeding up is possible, any task which calls for the processing of symbolic material at speed is likely to cause them difficulty. In most cases, too, there will be problems with remembering times, dates, appointments, etc., and for some it is difficult to remember and reproduce items in a series such as the months of the year.

Today, however, it has become widely recognised that dyslexics should be encouraged to 'think positive' and not to underestimate their abilities. Some of them can be extremely creative and many are gifted in art, architecture, engineering and the like.

This imbalance of skills is reflected in the way in which dyslexics perform at mathematics. Mathematics calls for many different kinds of ability. In general, dyslexics tend to be slow at certain basic aspects of mathematics – learning multiplication tables, adding up columns of figures, etc. – but once they have understood the symbols they can show profound understanding and may be extremely creative. It is therefore crucially important to distinguish the dyslexic child from the slow learning child, whose educational needs are very different.

Readers wishing for an overview of the field, with information as to where more detailed evidence can be found, may like to consult Miles and Miles (1999). For a series of papers reflecting some of the areas currently being researched we recommend Fawcett and Nicolson (eds) (2001). For reports of the many different stresses experienced by dyslexics, readers may like to consult Miles (ed.) (2004).

It is now established beyond reasonable doubt – something which had earlier been suspected but was supported only by circumstantial evidence – that the manifestations of dyslexia have a physical (constitutional) basis. This was confirmed in the 1980s by post-mortem examination of the brains of those known to have been dyslexic in their lifetime, and, more recently, by ever-more sophisticated brain-scan techniques.

Awareness that dyslexia has a physical basis is important for teachers for a number of reasons. In particular, if one knows that a child is struggling to compensate for a constitutionally caused weakness, one will be much more hesitant to accuse that child of laziness or lack of effort.

The most widely accepted explanation of the manifestations of dyslexia, though by common consent it does not explain all of them, is that dyslexics have difficulty with phonology – that is, with the remembering and ordering of speech sounds. It follows that – at least in the case of the English language – letter-sound correspondences need to be taught slowly and systematically; and to aid memorising the teaching has to be multisensory, that is, to involve as many senses as possible. Thus the pupil is encouraged to look carefully at what he has written, to listen carefully to the sound of the word (and note the number of syllables), to pay attention to his mouth movements in saying the word and to his hand movements in writing it. As will be seen later in this book, a multisensory approach is also essential in teaching dyslexics to understand mathematics.[1]

SOME INFORMAL OBSERVATIONS

I begin this section by reporting some of the observations made by myself and others over the years. My central aim is to illustrate the incongruities found in the performance of dyslexics in the area of mathematics; some of them can have all sorts of ingenious and creative ideas, and yet have extreme difficulty over learning multiplication tables and other basic number facts. Some of them in fact show their ingenuity in finding 'ways round' – compensatory strategies – when knowledge of the required number fact is not automatic.

Problems over left and right

I tested Joan for suspected dyslexia. She was aged 16, and was hoping to go to university. She showed many indicators of dyslexia on the Bangor Dyslexia Test (Miles 1982, 1997), including an incongruous failure at 'three digits reversed' – when asked to say '3-7-1' backwards she said '1-3-7'. Yet on the Terman Merrill intelligence test she passed three items out of four at Superior Adult I and three items out of four at Superior Adult II. My colleague, Barbara Large, reported to me that during subsequent tuition she was given the sums: $103 - 52$ and $36 - 27$. She produced the following:

$$\begin{array}{r} 103 \\ 52 \\ \hline 672 \end{array}$$

Her reasoning was: 'Five from one won't go, so borrow ten and turn the one into eleven – five from eleven leaves six. Pay back the one so that the middle figure in the 103 becomes nine – two from nine leaves seven. Pay back again so that the three in the 103 becomes two, and subtract zero from it – so six-seven-two'.

Joan had clearly learned something about 'borrowing' and 'paying back', but with no real understanding, and no awareness of the approximate order of magnitude of the correct answer. One of her basic mistakes was to start the subtraction sum on the left and not on the right – and we know that uncertainty over left and right is very common among dyslexics.

In the next sum she tried to adopt similar procedures and was completely defeated.

What she wrote was:

$$\begin{array}{r} 36 \\ 27 \\ \hline 1? \end{array}$$

She could take two from three but how was she to take seven from six?

Any dyslexic who is uncertain over left and right has to come to terms with the fact that in three of the four arithmetical operations (multiplication, addition and subtraction) one has to start on the right, whereas in the case of the fourth (division) one has to start on the left.

Farnham-Diggory (1978) also cites a case where confusion between left and right led to problems. Although 'he solved mental problems by clever regrouping strategies ... Ralph's written compositions were seriously in error. He lined up numbers from left to right, as in

$$
\begin{array}{r}
23 \\
+5 \\
\hline
73
\end{array}
$$

He did not know how to carry; for example, given

$$
\begin{array}{r}
19 \\
+16
\end{array}
$$

he began to add from the left, doing $1 + 1 = 2$. Next he did $9 + 6 = 15$, which would have given him

$$
\begin{array}{r}
19 \\
+\ 16 \\
\hline
215
\end{array}
$$

which would have given him 215, but somehow – it is not clear how – he realised that 215 contained too many digits. His solution was simply to ignore the 5! This then gave him an answer of 21'.

I came across an interesting example of how left–right confusion can affect one's judgement of number. This goes back to, the days when petrol was 74p per gallon. I was told by the parents of a 15-year-old that on the journey to my assessment he had looked towards a petrol pump and said: 'Gosh! That petrol's cheap – only 47p'.

Compensatory strategies

Some of the remarkable behaviour which I have observed in dyslexics seems to be the consequence of their trying to devise their own compensatory strategies. If one does not have the number facts readily available there are still ways of compensating. My first example is that of a girl aged 10 who, when asked what was '19 take away 7', produced the response shown in Figure 1.1.

Her procedure was to make 19 marks on the paper, then separate out seven of them, and then count up the remainder, which gave her the correct

Figure 1.1 Response to 19 take away 7

answer, 12. Her procedure is interesting because most children aged 10 would have been able to give the answer 'in one'.

In a school exercise book belonging to a dyslexic boy whom I will call John (I have no record of his exact age), I found as shown in Figure 1.2.

I do not know his exact strategy, but I suspect he may have drawn the dividing lines after each group of two marks and then written in the numbers. Only when he had got as far as 46 was he able to count ahead and, presumably, come up with the answer 50. The figures $2\overline{)100}$ in the bottom right corner may have been an attempt to oblige the teacher by doing as he was told, but why his teacher had asked him to start the sum in this way was clearly lost on him.

How many two's are there in one hundred?

```
 1   2   3   4   5   6   7   8   9  10  11 12  13
11| 11| 11| 11| 11| 11| 11| 11| 11| 11| 11| 11| 11|

14  15 16  17  18  19  20  21  22 23  24  25 26  27
11| 11| 11| 11| 11| 11| 11| 11| 11| 11| 11| 11| 11| 11|

28  29 30  31  32  33  34 35  36  37  38  39 40  41
11| 11| 11| 11| 11| 11| 11| 11| 11| 11| 11| 11| 11| 11|

42  43  44  45 46
11| 11| 11| 11| 11| 11| 11| 11| 11|
```

$2\overline{)100}$

Figure 1.2 How many two's are there in one hundred?

John had made a valiant effort, which one cannot but admire. However, although in general I am reluctant to interfere when dyslexics produce their own ingenious ways of doing things, in John's case I would have sounded him as to whether he was interested in a less time consuming and more labour saving way of arriving at the answer. If he knew that there are five twos in ten and that 20 is 10 × 2, 30 is 10 × 3, etc. he might have arrived at the answer, 50, more quickly and with less effort.

It is my experience that many dyslexic children need to use marks on paper or concrete aids at an age where most of their non-dyslexic peers find this unnecessary. It seems as though in many cases the memorising of number facts does not come easily or automatically. It also makes sense to suppose that where there are regularities in the number system such memorising is easier.

Many of the contributors to this book will be pointing out the usefulness of algorithms – that is, rules of procedure – in those situations where one does not have a number fact immediately available. My suggestion is that dyslexics who resort to marks on paper or to counting on their fingers at an age when most of their peers find this unnecessary, do so because they need an algorithm – and there is one unfailing algorithm that they can use, namely that the numbers go up in ones!

I owe to my colleague, Anne Henderson, the following remarkable example of a compensatory strategy.

David was asked to multiply 532 by 8. The following is a record of his comments:

> Think of 8 as 10 and of 532 as 500. 500 times 10 is 5000. But this is two lots of 500 too big. 500 doubled is 1000; 5000 − 1000 is 4000. Think of 32 as 30 – I don't know my 8× table – only my 5× table, so 5 × 8 is 40; 10 × 8 is 40 doubled = 80. I need three lots of 10s in 30, 80 doubled is 160 = 20 × 8, therefore 160 + 80 = 30 × 8 = 240. 8 doubled is 16. So the answer is 4000 + 240 + 16, which is 4256.

This answer is correct! – and, given that he did not know his 8× table, is a remarkable tribute to David's ingenuity.

Losing track

Another characteristic of dyslexics (to which we shall be returning in the next section) is that they are liable to 'lose track' of where they are; for example, in reciting times tables they are liable to produce such questions as, 'Was it six sevens I was up to?'. A likely explanation seems to be that, in comparison with non-dyslexics their memories are more likely to become overloaded. My colleague, Ann Cooke, told me of a boy who, when the task involved holding in mind several things at once, commented 'I haven't got enough think left'. Here is an account of a dyslexic businessman who experienced this difficulty – and he showed me how he had devised a strategy for getting round it.

A dyslexic businessman who was in the meat trade continually found himself having to add up columns of figures. On one occasion, the requirement was to add 7, 3, 12, 22, 43 and 37. Instead of writing all the figures in a column and adding them up (as most of us would have done), he set them out as follows:

```
         7
         3                    1 0
      ......
       1 2
       2 2                    3 4
      ......
       4 3
       3 7                    8 0
      ......                ........
                             1 2 4
```

As a result of this compensatory strategy, he could arrive at the correct answer without ever having to hold in mind more than three numbers.

The incongruous balance of skills

I have often been amazed by the ingenuity of some of these compensatory strategies. This is the positive side of dyslexia – it takes a clever and creative person to think of them! It is not therefore surprising that among dyslexics we find some who were highly successful at mathematics – those aspects of mathematics which call for creativity rather than the rote learning of number bonds. Dr Turner Ellis in Chapter 8 cites the case of Kalvis Jansons (see Jansons 1988) who became a university lecturer in mathematics. Steeves (1983: 141) cites the case of a 9-year-old boy, two years behind grade level at reading and spelling and only 'average' on a mathematics test, who, having been shown some graph paper, cried out excitedly, after no more than 12 seconds, 'that there were 28,000 little squares on his sheet of paper'. Griffiths (1980: 50–3) cites the case of a university lecturer in physics who in middle age was still found to be unsure of his $6\times$ table – yet it is clearly essential for a successful physicist to be able to operate with advanced mathematical concepts.

I myself have come across many dyslexics over the years who have displayed a similar imbalance of skills – high ability to understand and operate with difficult concepts, but with an inability to remember what seem to the rest of us to be the simplest of number facts. I used to give the Terman Merrill intelligence test (Terman and Merrill 1960), which often gave some very informative results. In one of the items the subject is told that he has been sent to a river and given two cans for holding water, a 5-pint can and a 9-pint can: filling the 9-pint can first he must bring back exactly 13 pints of water. An 11-year-old whom I was testing had no difficulty in grasping the essentials of the problem and realised that the 5-pint can had to be filled from the 9-pint can and then emptied so as to make room for what was left in the 9-pint can. The 'difficult' part for him – he eventually succeeded – was working out that $9 + 4 = 13$! I had a similar experience when a 16-year-old was attempting the Terman Merrill 'tree' item, which is at the third (top) grade of 'Superior Adult'. In successive years, the tree grows from eight feet to 12, then to 18 and then to 27 feet, and the subject is asked how tall the tree will be at the end of the fourth year. The problem involves, at least implicitly, the ability to operate with the concept of acceleration, the successive increases $(+4, +6, +9)$ allowing for an answer of either 40 or 40.5 according to whether one adds or multiplies. According to the test instructions the subject is not permitted to use pencil and paper, but since memorising the figures 4, 5, and 6 would be very hard for a dyslexic, I used to waive this requirement – a legitimate procedure provided one does not go on to cite an IQ figure in the traditional sense.[2] One of my subjects, aged 16, grasped the essentials of the problem perfectly well but gave an incorrect answer because he mistakenly believed that $27 - 18$ was 11. Dr Ann Dowker, in Chapter 9 of this book, reports having encountered something similar.

One of my students, who obtained a very creditable honours degree in Psychology – a course which demands a thorough understanding of the concepts used in statistics, reported that she still did not know immediately that 6 plus 7 was 13, but 'had a strategy for working it out'.

Particularly interesting, in this connection, is the case of a student described by Cooke (2002) who came to university as a virtual non-reader but who nevertheless obtained an honours degree in Psychology with a similar, highly demanding, statistical content. Though scoring at average level or above on most items of the WAIS (Wechsler Adult Intelligence Scale), on the Digit Span sub-test she had a score of 2, which is massively below the expected average score of 10. Her dyslexic difficulties extended into arithmetic: she even had difficulty in learning the names of the numerals – in her own words, she 'didn't know what they were called'. However, she was still able to grasp mathematical concepts, and without this understanding it would not have been possible for her to obtain her degree.

Newby (2004) has suggested that because of the stress imposed on dyslexics in having to learn basic literacy and numeracy these skills should not necessarily be routinely taught in the early stages. He suggests that dyslexics should come to them gradually and for occasions when they need them. West (1997) has argued that it is a fault of our educational system that these skills are over-valued at the expense of originality and creativity; many of the skills required for literacy and numeracy can nowadays be carried out much more efficiently by computers.

SYSTEMATIC COMPARISONS

Three studies will now be reported in which attempts have been made at systematic comparisons between dyslexics and non-dyslexics in the area of mathematics. Without such comparisons, it is not possible to be sure whether, or to what extent, some mathematical difficulties are distinctive to dyslexics or how far such difficulties are shared by non-dyslexics also.

Steeves (1983)

A particularly interesting pioneer study was carried out by Steeves (1983). Her subjects were 54 dyslexic boys between the ages of 10 and 14 years. She divided them into four groups: (i) 'dyslexics high' (DH), that is, dyslexics with a high score on the Standard Progressive Matrices (SPM) test (Raven 1958); (ii) 'dyslexics average' (DA), that is, dyslexics with an average score on the SPM; (iii) 'non-dyslexics high' (NH), that is, non-dyslexics in a high or advanced class for mathematics; and (iv) 'non-dyslexics average' (NA), that is, non-dyslexics in an average class for mathematics. The DH group were found on testing to be at the same level on the SPM as the NH group. On a test of school mathematics, however, they scored lower than the NH group and were on a level with the NA group, while on the Wechsler Memory test they scored lower than both the non-dyslexic groups. The DA group were on a level with the NA group on SPM score but below them on the school mathematics test and particularly far below on the Wechsler Memory test.

On the basis of these results Steeves is in no doubt that some dyslexics can be gifted mathematically, and, indeed, if this were not so, it is hard to see how the DH group could have been on a level with an 'average' group of non-dyslexics on a school mathematics test. Since, however, a high score on the SPM is widely agreed to constitute evidence for mathematical potential, the question arises as to why the DH group scored lower than the NH group on the mathematics test. Steeves convincingly argues that, since they scored highly on the SPM, any weaknesses that they showed could not have been due to lack of maturity, visual weakness, spatial problems, perceptual confusion or sequencing difficulties. Where they, in fact, came down was on the Wechsler Memory Test, and here they obtained lower scores even than the NA group, despite their higher scores on the SPM. Her explanation – which is coherent with what is known about dyslexia from other sources – is that, despite their high potential, they were handicapped at mathematics by those parts of the subject, which call for memorising ability.

Miles (1993)

In a study reported by Miles (1993) 132 dyslexics between the ages of 7 and 18 years, and 132 controls, matched as far as possible for age and intelligence, were asked to recite either the 4× table (those aged 7 and 8) and or the 6, 7, and 8 times tables (the others). A child was said to have 'difficulty' not only if they made mistakes but if they 'lost their way', for instance by asking 'How many sixes had I got to?', or if they corrected themselves, went back to an earlier 'anchor point', or broke into the 'wrong' table. In this study 90 per cent of the dyslexics aged 7 and 8, 96 per cent of those between 9 and 12, and 85 per cent of those between 13 and 18, had 'difficulty' in the specified sense, whereas the corresponding percentage figures for the controls were 71, 51 and 53. These percentage figures suggest that reciting tables without stumbling is hard for many children. More important, the high percentage figures for the dyslexics seem hard to square with the claim sometimes made by Joffe (1990) that only 60 per cent of dyslexics have difficulty with mathematics. It seems more correct to say that a very great majority – perhaps even 100 per cent – have difficulty with certain aspects of mathematics. Examination of chapter 16 of Miles (1993) reveals some very remarkable performances on the part of the dyslexics when reciting tables. It is possible that one reason why they 'lose their way' is that they were asked to include the 'preamble' ('one six is', 'two sixes are', etc.) and that it was the extra 'load' on their memories that caused some of the problems. Although the data were collected at a time when rote learning of tables was possibly more common than it is to-day, they still illustrate how dyslexics can fail when too severe a memory load is imposed on them and how, for dyslexics, the learning of new number facts becomes automatic, if at all, only after considerable practice. Readers may also like to consult this book, which discusses some of the special strategies needed by dyslexics for successful addition and subtraction.[3]

Miles, Haslum and Wheeler (2001)

A study has also been carried out on the mathematical abilities of dyslexic and non-dyslexic 10 year olds (Miles *et al.* 2001). A test containing 72 mathematical items was given to some 12,000 children as part of the British Births Cohort Study (1970). Most aspects of school mathematics were represented – number, time, length, area, volume, capacity, money, graphs, statistics, mass, shape, angles and co-ordinates.

One of the comparisons made was that between the group believed to contain the largest number of dyslexics ($N = 269$) and the group containing the smallest number of dyslexics ($N = 6,333$). On the basis of two intelligence tests from the British Ability Scales (Elliot *et al.* 1979, 1983) it was found that the groups were approximately of the same intelligence, but in spite of this the group containing the dyslexics obtained lower pass rates on virtually all the 72 items. What was particularly interesting was that on some items the difference in percentage pass rate was quite small whereas in other cases it was very large. Thus when the children were asked to add one half to one half, 84 per cent of the non-dyslexic group answered correctly, compared with 77 per cent of the dyslexic group. In contrast, when they were asked to multiply 137 by 7, the pass rates were 77 and 38 per cent. This last sum required not only a knowledge of the $7\times$ table, but the ability to hold in mind both the numbers themselves and the successive stages of the calculation. The results of this study suggest that success in mathematics is at least possible for dyslexics, but that for many of them the actual mechanics of calculation presents problems. It seems that repetitive calculation exercises are not the answer. There is therefore a very good case for exposing dyslexics to the creative aspects of mathematics.

THE NEED FOR MULTISENSORY TEACHING

Introduction

There can be no doubt that the same structured multisensory methods that have long been known to be effective in the teaching of literacy (see e.g. Hornsby and Miles 1980) are also highly desirable in the teaching of mathematics. The programme needs to have a structure, so that each step is thoroughly learned – and, indeed, over-learned – before the teacher proceeds to the next one. Because of limitations in what a dyslexic pupil can 'take in' at any one time, the steps need to be very small ones; otherwise he may miss an important stage in the argument. A multisensory approach can be achieved by the use of concrete aids, such as Dienes blocks and Cuisinaire rods.

The Flynn multimedia calculator

An interesting way of achieving a structured multisensory approach has been devised by Flynn (1998); it takes the form of a multimedia calculator devised so as to take account of the distinctive needs of dyslexics. This programme, which is available on CD Rom, creates a 'virtual reality' in which symbols such as '+' and '×' appear as well as numerals. The names of the numerals are spoken by a voice, as well as the names of the operations ('add', 'divide', etc.), and the user can watch the operations actually taking place and noting how the blocks change according to what numbers are being multiplied, divided, added or subtracted. It is possible for the user not only to watch things happen but to press keys so as to *make* them happen.[4] Such a device has many advantages over the pocket calculator, which, though it can save labour if properly used, is something of a hazard for dyslexics; not only is there the risk that they may press the wrong key, but if they have not been taught to estimate they may not be able to tell if their answer is of the right order of magnitude, and, most importantly, the calculator does little to help them to understand mathematical operations.

Gypsy multiplication

I end this section by passing on a procedure – probably familiar already to many teachers – which may be of help to those who do not easily remember the 6, 7 and 8 times tables. The procedure in fact works for the $9\times$ and $10\times$ also, but the $10\times$ is unlikely to present any problems, while the $9\times$ can be remembered if one notes that the two digits always add up to nine – zero-nine, one-eight, two-seven, etc. In the case of the present technique it is assumed that the typical dyslexic will have no problem with the $5\times$ and that if the tables below five are not immediately known the numbers are small enough to make calculation manageable. (There may be problems if the method is used with dyspraxic pupils because of their poor motor control.)

The procedure is for the pupil to imagine two hands, set out as in Figure 1.3.

Each thumb represents 6, each index finger 7, each middle finger 8, each fourth finger 9 and each little finger 10.

How, then, would one multiply seven by eight? Place the index finger of the left hand (7) opposite the middle finger of the right hand (8) and count the number of fingers, as far as the two touching fingers, on the near side of the body. This gives the tens column – in the present case, 5. Then multiply together the fingers on the far side of the body – in this case 3×2,

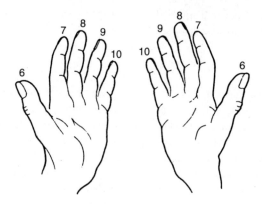

Figure 1.3 Gypsy multiplication

which gives the figure for the units as 6. The answer therefore is 56. (There is a complication in that for 6 × 6, four times four (= 16) has to be added, and for 7×6, three times four (= 12) has to be added.) The advantage of this method is that it requires no immediate knowledge of any product containing a number higher than four. For interest, a proof of the procedure is given in the Appendix.

OTHER DEVELOPMENTAL ANOMALIES

Introduction

Since the publication of the first edition of this book a number of diagnostic labels have become increasingly current. The relevant ones for purposes of this chapter are attention deficit hyperactivity disorder (ADHD), dyspraxia and dyscalculia.

Some Education Authorities tell us that they are reluctant to 'label' children because this makes them 'different'. I have never been able to understand this view. Children *are* different, and the alternative to a correct diagnostic label is an incorrect one, as when a dyslexic child is stigmatised as 'lazy', 'careless' or 'dumbo'.

That the diagnostic label 'dyslexia' is of value cannot now be doubted. That the manifestations have a neurological basis, that they persist, and that systematic multisensory teaching is normally called for – these points are not in dispute. That the terms dyspraxia and ADHD represent genuine conditions is also not in dispute. In the case of ADHD and dyscalculia, however, though the existence of manifestations which some people *call* 'dyscalculia' is not in dispute, the theoretical issues arising from these two terms are far from straightforward.

ADHD

Detailed discussion of ADHD is beyond the scope of this chapter. Some critical comments will be found in Reason (1999) and Fawcett (2003). In brief, the description 'ADHD' has been used to describe the condition of those individuals who act very impulsively and – perhaps because of their physical make-up – cannot easily control their impulses. Some of these individuals may also have problems of attention and concentration. Relevant to our purposes is the fact that some children described as having ADHD may also have problems with calculation. In the USA, many of these children are put on Ritalin, but it remains an open question to what extent management by setting the right environmental conditions, for example making the lessons interesting and attractive, rather than using medication is the preferable treatment.

Dyspraxia

The central feature in dyspraxia is poor motor co-ordination. Not all dyspraxics have literacy problems, although many do. Nor are all dyslexics poorly co-ordinated – a dyslexic girl whom I assessed some years ago has grown up to become a highly successful ballet dancer! However, there is considerable overlap (or 'co-morbidity') between the two conditions.

Dyspraxia, incidentally, is sometimes referred to as 'developmental co-ordination disorder' (DCD) and in the past was known as the 'clumsy child' syndrome, There is less research evidence on dyspraxia in comparison with dyslexia, but a sizeable amount has been learned on the basis of practical experience (see e.g. Thomson *et al.* 2000).

There has been a major development in the field as a result of a book recently published by Yeo (2003). We owe to Yeo a comprehensive and authoritative account of her experiences in teaching mathematics to both dyslexic and dyspraxic children at the primary school level.

Among the many exciting ideas in her book, Yeo has provided a careful and detailed examination of those arithmetical procedures which she believes will come most easily to dyslexic and dyspraxic children. These procedures are what she calls 'big value' methods. For instance, if two 2-digit numbers have to be added, say 36 and 38, the 'big value' method in this case involves what she calls 'partitioning'; this means that the sum is partitioned into small steps, in which (in this case) 32 is treated as 30, to with 6 added; 38 is similarly treated as 30, with 8 added. The two 30s are then added to give 60, and the 8+6, to give 14 · · · 60 and 4 are 74. The children are encouraged to work horizontally and not vertically, and there is no need for them to hold in mind which numbers need to be 'carried' – something which dyslexics find very far from easy.

She suggests that in most respects dyslexic and dyspraxic children share the same difficulties over number. In a few respects, however, she has found them to be different: 'While it is fair to say that the majority of dyslexic children have difficulty remembering rote-learning and verbally encoded facts we cannot make such a general statement about dyspraxic children'. She goes on to say that while many can learn, it is often without understanding (Yeo 2003: 321–2).

Dyscalculia

The term 'dyscalculia' has come to the fore in British education as a result of a circular on numeracy from the Department for Education and Science (DfES), which refers to both dyslexia and dyscalculia. 'Dyscalculia is a condition which affects the ability to acquire arithmetical skills. Dyscalculic learners may have difficulty understanding simple number concepts, lack an intuitive grasp of numbers, and may have problems learning number facts and procedures. Even if they produce a correct answer or use a correct method, they may do so hesitantly and without confidence. Very little is known about the prevalence of dyscalculia, its causes or treatment. Purely dyscalculic learners who have difficulties only with number will have cognitive and language abilities in the normal range and may excel in non-mathematical subjects. It is more likely that difficulties with numeracy accompany the language difficulties of dyslexia' (DfES circular, p. 2).

On this showing, dyscalculia is a very basic problem with numeracy which is not simply the consequence of the dyslexic problems already described in this chapter – inability to hold in mind a sequence of operations, left–right confusion and difficulty in acquiring responses that are automatic.

Most of us would agree that there is no point in using a fancy '*dys*' label if one means only that the person is 'not very good' at something. Plenty of people are not very good at mathematics without meriting the (perhaps rather exotic) label 'dyscalculia'. '*Dys*' labels are appropriate only if there is a specific handicap or disability; and one speaks of 'disability' only if the difficulties persist and are not easy to remediate and where there is a known or inferred neurological basis. Unless this is the case, any '*dys*' label is no more than a high faluting way of saying something which one could perfectly well say in plain English!

The theoretical issue over dyscalculia (and, indeed, over other '*dys*' words) is where to 'lump' (i.e. to group phenomena together) and where to 'split' (i.e. classify as different and separate). In the present context the question is whether dyslexia and dyscalculia should be classified separately as two separate syndromes, or whether all the mathematical difficulties experienced by dyslexics are part and parcel of their dyslexia.

In general, as knowledge increases, researchers find it necessary to revise the boundaries which they mark for classification purposes, and make new decisions as to where to 'lump' and where to 'split'. In this particular case, we need to await the results of further research before we can be sure whether dyslexia and dyscalculia should be treated as two separate syndromes.

The proposal made by the DfES is that the word 'dyscalculia' should be used only when there are no accompanying literacy difficulties. That such cases can be found is not in serious doubt (Butterworth 1999, 2003; Malmer 2000; Ramaa and Gowramma 2002).

I myself described a small number of such cases at a conference a few years ago (Miles 2000). They included an account of a university professor and his daughter, along with an account of a young musician, Helen Poole, who has also written her own story (Poole 2001). Reports on the first two cases have not so far been published.

Professor X was a Professor of History with many distinguished publications to his name. He had no difficulties in either reading or spelling. However, he had a real dread of mental arithmetic, which he found extremely difficult. He had some problems with the reading of music, always preferring to play by ear. He failed 'school certificate' maths and had to re-take the exam. He had difficulty in retaining telephone numbers and even in remembering his own car registration number. He never forgot a person's handwriting. Though forgetful and careless with his own possessions, he always knew where in the house to find a book. He was extremely methodical in making research notes in spite of the appearance of disorder.

Joyce, the daughter of Professor X, was an early reader and never had any difficulty with spelling. However, reading music was always a problem. She was late in learning to tell the time, reading twenty-five past one as twenty-five to eleven. Arithmetic became an insurmountable hurdle, and she failed the 11+ exam on account of this but was admitted to the Grammar School at the headmistress's discretion. Maths continued to be a nightmare.

Helen spoke early, although tying shoelaces was a problem. She was unable to learn 'times tables' as a child – 'mother tried every method possible'. However, she obtained grade Bs at 'A' level in English and French, as well as further B and C grades, In her own words, 'I have always been a very advanced speaker and reader'. When she was given the Bangor Dyslexia Test

(Miles 1982, 1997), there were what seemed to be clear positive indicators of dyslexia, including uncertainty over 'left' and 'right' and poor memory for the recall of digits both in forwards and reverse order. Her father was dyslexic, and, overall, her tally of five-and-a-half positive indicators out of a possible 10 is right outside normal limits for a non-dyslexic of that age and background. She needed all kinds of special strategies in order to do calculation, and though a gifted musician who could play several instruments, she had difficulty with musical notation and with playing or singing back a melody.

In all these three cases one must conclude that there was a definite disability in mathematics, not just that they were 'not very good' at it. This is shown not only by the persistence of the difficulties and their resistance to remediation, but also by the fact that there appears to be a familial – and presumably genetic – factor at work.

Although Helen described herself as 'dyscalculic', it is possible that she should more properly be regarded as a somewhat unusual case of dyslexia. Evidence that there can be dyslexia without *severe* literacy problems has been provided by Miles *et al.* (2003); and there are no grounds for supposing that Helen had the severe difficulties over number described in the DfES document; when she played her various musical instruments there was no indication that counting the time was any major problem for her.

A view basically similar to that of the DfES document has been put forward by Butterworth (1999) who has also published a 'Dyscalculia Screener' (Butterworth 2003), aimed at discovering those who, because of a basic neurological deficit, have difficulty in acquiring what he calls 'numerosity'.

The tests in the Screener involve counting of dots, comparison of number sizes and some simple calculations. Because Butterworth was concerned to discover how *quickly* the subjects could respond, all items were timed, with the subjects responding by pressing a button either on the left or on the right according to the question asked. In the dot counting, task arrays of up to nine dots are presented randomly on the screen, along with a numeral and the subject has to say if the number of dots does or does not agree with the numeral. Then, if, say, there were eight random dots on the screen and the numeral 8 was presented the subject would have to indicate 'yes'. In the comparison of number size, pairs of numerals appear on the screen and the subject has to press the appropriate button to indicate which is the larger. In some cases the numerals are of different font size, for example, 7 and 2. (This is a variant of what is called a 'Stroop' task, where, for instance, the word RED might be presented, written in *green* ink.) There are also addition and multiplication sums; for instance, one of the sums is '3 + 8 = 12', and a measure is taken of the time needed by the subject to press the 'false' button.

Evidence relevant to Butterworth's view will be found in a paper by Isaacs *et al.* (2001). Their subjects were survivors of pre-term birth (gestation period 30 weeks or less). The authors report: 'We have been able to demonstrate that there is an area in the left parietal lobe where children without a deficit in calculation ability have more grey matter than those who do have this deficit.... (p. 1701).... The children all had well developed literacy skills and no apparent language deficits ... The implication of these results is that the integrity of the left intraparietal sulcul area is necessary for the appropriate levels of calculation ability in these children. However, the results should not be interpreted to mean that this area is the only important region for calculation. A whole network of regions could participate in normal processing' (p. 1706).

Butterworth's concept of an innate 'number module' is a novel one and has not yet been fully evaluated. There are, however, problems with his Screener, which should perhaps be mentioned. Given that slowness in responding could be indicative of a deficient 'number nodule', it could also be indicative of a number of other things. The person being tested has to read instructions on the screen, and, for a dyslexic, any reading in test conditions may cause panic. Quick responding also calls for a sure sense of 'left' and 'right', and this, too, is something which may cause problems to dyslexics. They may also be slowed down because of lack of immediate knowledge of number facts, particularly in multiplication, in comparison with their non-dyslexic peers. These considerations do not, of course, establish that Butterworth's hypothesis of a deficient number module is mistaken but only that the Dyscalculia Screener as it stands does not adequately differentiate dyslexics from dyscalculics.

One final paper on dyscalculia requires mention, that which reports two studies by Ramaa and Gowramma (2002). Like Malmer and Butterworth, these authors took the view that no child should count as dyscalculic if the arithmetical problems were accompanied by literacy problems. They also considered it necessary to exclude those children whose arithmetical failure could have been attributed to lack of support in the home. One of the two studies, that by Ramaa, included tests of number concept, the four arithmetical operations, and arithmetical reasoning; the other relied on exclusionary criteria. Although the investigations by Butterworth, on the one hand, and those by Ramaa and Gowramma on the other, each claimed to be studying 'dyscalculia', the differences in their procedures are such as to make direct comparison difficult.

The subjects in the Indian studies were drawn from Primary Schools in Mysore, some of the instruction being through the medium of the Kannada language and some through the medium of English. Ramaa's pool of subjects comprised 251 children, of whom 15 (5.98 per cent), met the criteria for being dyscalculic, while the figures for Gowramma were 78 out of 1,408 (5.54 per cent). The two percentage figures are strikingly similar, even though there was an interval of almost 10 years between the two studies. If dyscalculia in their sense is a worldwide phenomenon (as dyslexia is believed to be), then it is possible that, if similar criteria were used, similar percentage figures would be found in other parts of the world.

Firm conclusions, however, about the existence and nature of dyscalculia must await further research.

NOTES

1. See, in particular, chapter 12 of Miles and Miles (1999) for a review of the many different teaching programmes now on the market.
2. The notion of an IQ figure in the case of a dyslexic adult or dyslexic child is extremely problematic (compare Miles 1996).
3. The Bangor Dyslexia Test, on which these findings are based, is obtainable from Learning Development Aids, Duke St., Wisbech, Cambridge, England PE 13 2AE (tel.: 01945 463441 <www.ldalearning.com>).
4. The CD Rom may be obtained from Inclusive Technology <www.inclusive.co.uk> (tel.: 01457 819790).

REFERENCES

Butterworth, B. (1999) *The Mathematical Brain*, London, Macmillan.
Butterworth, B. (2003) *Dyscalculia Screener*, London, NFER-Nelson.
Cooke, E.A. (2002) 'Case study: a virtual non-reader achieves a degree', *Dyslexia: An International Journal of Research and Practice*, 8(2), 102–15.
DfES (2001) *The National Numeracy Strategy: Guidance to Support Pupils With Dyslexia and Dyscalculia*, DfES 2051 212001.
Elliot, C.D., Murray, D.J. and Pearson, L.S. (1979, 1983) *The British Ability Scales*, Windsor, NFER-Nelson.
Farnham-Diggory, S. (1978) *Learning Disabilities*, London, Fontana.
Fawcett, A.J. (2004) 'Individual case studies and recent research', in T.R. Miles (ed.) *Dyslexia and Stress* (2nd edn), London, Whurr.
Fawcett, A.J. and Nicolson, R.I. (eds) (2001) *Dyslexia: Theory and Good Practice*, London, Whurr.
Flynn, S.J.O. (1998) *The Mulitmedia Interactive Calculator*, Inclusive Technology Ltd. (Saddleworth Business Centre, Delph, Oldham OL3 5DF.)
Griffiths, J.M. (1980) 'Basic arithmetic processes in the dyslexic child'. MEd. dissertation, University of Wales.
Hornsby, B. and Miles, T.R. (1980) 'The effects of a dyslexia-centred teaching programme', *British Journal of Educational Psychology*, 50, 236–42.

Isaacs, C.J., Edmunds, J., Lucas, A. and Gadian, D.G. (2001) 'Calculation difficulties in children of very low birthweight: a neural correlate', *Brain*, 1241, 1701–7.

Jansons, K.M. (1988) 'A personal view of dyslexia and of thought without language', in L. Weiskrantz (ed.) *Thought Without Language*, Oxford, Oxford University Press.

Joffe, L.S. (1990) 'The mathematical aspects of dyslexia: a recap of general issues and some implications for teaching', *Links*, 15(2), 7–10.

Malmer, G. (2000) 'Mathematics and dyslexia: an overlooked connection', *Dyslexia: An International Journal of Research and Practice*, 6(4), 223–30.

Miles, T.R. (1982, 1997) *The Bangor Dyslexia Test*, Wisbech, Cambridge, Learning Development Aids.

Miles, T.R. (1993) *Dyslexia: The Pattern of Difficulties*, London, Whurr.

Miles, T.R. (1996) 'Do dyslexic children have IQs?', *Dyslexia: A International Journal of Research and Practice*, 2(4), 175–8.

Miles, T.R. (2000) 'Dyslexia minus' Paper delivered at Gregynog Hall, Wales in April 2000.

Miles, T.R. (ed.) (2004) *Dyslexia and Stress* (2nd edn), London, Whurr.

Miles T.R. and Miles, E. (1999) *Dyslexia: A Hundred Years On*, Ballmoor, Bucks, Open University Press.

Miles, T.R., Haslum, M.N. and Wheeler, T.J. (2001) 'Mathematical difficulties of 10-year-old dyslexic children', *Annals of Dyslexia*, 51, 299–331.

Miles, T.R., Wheeler, T.J. and Haslum, M.N. (2003) 'Dyslexia without severe literacy problems', *Annals of Dyslexia*, 53, 340–54.

Newby, M. (2004) 'Dyslexia without stress', in T.R. Miles (ed.) *Dyslexia and Stress* (2nd edn), London, Whurr, pp. 123–30.

Poole, H. (2001) 'My maths, my music and my dyscalculia', in T.R. Miles and J. Westcombe (eds) *Music and Dyslexia: Opening New Doors*, London, Whurr.

Ramaa, S. and Gowramma, I.P. (2002) 'A systematic procedure for identifying dyscalculic children in India', *Dyslexia: An International Journal of Research and Practice*, 8(2), 67–85.

Raven, J.C. (1958) *Standard Progressive Matrices*, London, H.K. Lewis.

Reason, R. (1990) 'ADHD: a psychological response to an evolving concept', *Journal of Learning Disabilities*, 32, 85–91.

Steeves, K.J. (1983) 'Memory as a factor in the computational efficiency of dyslexic children with high abstract reasoning ability', *Annals of Dyslexia*, 33, 141–52.

Terman, L.M. and Merrill, M.A. (1960) *Stanford Binet Itelligence Scale*, London, H.K. Lewis.

Thomson, M.E., Nicolson, R.I., Flory, A.S., Payton, P., Winfield, M. and McCormick, M. (2000) 'Dyslexia and dyspraxia commentary', *Dyslexia: An International Journal of Research and Practice*, 6(3), 202–14.

West, T.G. (1997) *In the Mind's Eye. Visual Thinkers, Gifted People with Dyslexia, Computer Images and the Ironies of Creativity*, New York, Prometheus Books.

Yeo, D. (2003) *Dyslexia, Dyspraxia and Mathematics*, London, Whurr.

Chapter 2

Informal diagnosis and thinking style

S.J. Chinn

INTRODUCTION: THE USE OF STANDARDISED TESTS

Published tests for mathematics tend to be standardised (more common) or criterion referenced (less common), though they may be a combination (France 1979). A standardised test is usually used to provide an 'achievement age', that is to say, it compares the performance of a particular child on the test with the achievement of his peers on the same test. A criterion referenced test is designed to test if set criteria of achievement have been met, for example the ability to add two 3-digit numbers with 'carrying' in the tens.

Since the first edition of this book a number of new tests have been developed in the UK; the WRAT, the Wide Range Achievement Test (Jastak and Jastak 1993) has been published in its third edition, and national testing has been introduced into UK schools at ages 9 and 13 (in addition to the existing National General Certificate of Secondary Education examinations at 16 years). Consumers have a bigger choice of tests which means they have to make a choice, unless, of course they decide to give the child every test and create a serious case of mathematics anxiety.

Some of the new tests are targeted at small age ranges (Clausen-May *et al.* 2000), or even one particular year group (Vincent and Crumpler 2000). The Weschler test group have introduced the WOND (1996), the Weschler Objective Numerical Dimensions, which is restricted to use by psychologists. The new version of the WRAT has avoided my main criticism from the first edition of this book, by being presented in a much more user-friendly style with more space around each item and some lining off into sections. What teachers now have to do with this range of tests is to decide which suits their particular needs.

One of the key criteria for a maths test for dyslexic pupils is the 'look' of the test.

For example how closely spaced are the items? Closely written text may result in errors such as

22   Mary bought a record for
£1.69. How much change did   **50p**
she get from £2.00?   ....

23   Share £1.50 equally between
5 boys. How much did   30p
each one get?   ....

where the £1.50 from question 23 was subtracted from the £2.00 from the question above.

The questions teachers could ask to help in their selection of test appropriate to their needs may include:

- How complex is the language? Are you allowed to read the paper to the pupil? For example, a 15-year-old dyslexic pupil asked me if 'How many pence in a pound?' was 'How many peas in a pod?' taking him into the 'How many beans make five?' realm of fantasy maths.
- Are there diagrams to illustrate the problems? Our experience in Mark College suggests that dyslexic pupils do better in tests where there are appropriate diagrams.
- Then, for the more statistical facts, you might ask how many items for a one-year gain in maths age? (Most tests settle for 4 or 5.)
- What are the details of the sample used for the standardisation of the test? It is unlikely that the test has any standardisation based on dyslexic pupils.
- Does the test match your teaching programme?
- For pupils who have attention-span problems, which are rarely at their longest for dyslexic pupils, how long does the test take? Is it timed?
- And, to move to the main point of this the first part of this chapter, what diagnostic information can you extract from the test?
- For retesting, is there a parallel form?
- If you wish to monitor a pupil over a long period, then what is the age range of the test? Again our experience tells us that moving to a new test for the next age of pupils creates a break in the data needed for measuring progress.

A test can provide standardised data by comparing the total mark obtained by a child against charts of standardised data. The 'maths age' gives a broad indication of the depth of the child's problems in comparison to his peers. A closer examination of the items that the child got right and, more revealingly, the items he got wrong, his errors, will start to provide diagnostic information as to where the problems lie (Ashlock 1998). Borasi (1985) suggest that we should consider errors as windows by means of which we can get to know a person's conception of mathematics. There is no doubt that children can be very creative with their maths errors!

A classroom study by Chinn (1995) suggests that the errors made by dyslexics, in an untimed test, were not significantly different to those made by non-dyslexics, with one notable exception, the error of no-attempt. The hypothesis is that the dyslexic pupil looks at the item and, if he feels he may not get the right answer, then he just does not begin. These 'no-answers' may well be scattered throughout the test. Although information in itself, a 'no-answer' to a question may be for a number of reasons, for example, not knowing the basic facts to do the question (e.g. 6×7), or for being unable to recall the sequence of steps for the procedure (algorithm) to solve the question, or being unable to understand the question. This last reason may not even involve complex language, but simply be a matter of order as in, 'subtract 12 from 46' instead of 'from 46 subtract 12'. An ex-pupil of mine who went on to take a degree in mathematics said, 'I used to hate it when people said, if I had failed, "Never mind, you did your best" If I did my best then I didn't want to fail, so if I thought I might fail, then I wouldn't try'. And this from one of the most highly motivated pupils I have ever taught.

Some tests, for example the Mathematics Competency Test (Vernon *et al.* 1995), collect scores in categories to provide additional information, for example a weakness in Shape and Space items, so the basic score is now subdivided into areas of the curriculum. Further analysis may point to which level of difficulty of the topic creates the error. However perceptive the analysis, the restricted number of items in any test will create a limit to the extent of the diagnostic information that can be extracted, but, the extra information is so important. To quote Kaufman (2002) 'Be better than the test you use'.

The next stage of an assessment can use the information from the standardised test as a starting point for an informal and individually directed test protocol. Obviously the structure and content will depend on the age and achievement level of the child and on the information derived from the test. For example, the standardised test may have revealed a poor knowledge of basic facts or a problem when adding fractions.

It is not unusual for problems to be rooted very far back in the learning process. For example, not knowing the basic number bonds may handicap the pupil when attempting any addition sum. So adding $47 + 36$ requires him to know $7 + 6$ is 13. A simple strategy is to finger count, but that requires one-to-one correspondence and the awareness that the counting on starts at 8, not 7 and the ability to recognise 6 fingers so as to know when to stop counting.

This question also needs an understanding of place value if the answer is not to be computed as

$$
\begin{array}{r}
47 \\
+36 \\
\hline
713
\end{array}
$$

Once the informal testing begins, then the tester can ask the pupil to explain how he is 'doing the problem' or 'talk me through what you are doing'.

Setting up criterion referenced items for say, addition, could result in a very long test. For example, Wilson and Sadowski (1976) broke down the addition of whole numbers into 25 separate sequentially ordered steps. It could be argued that you would need more than one item per step to ensure a pattern of errors existed, making a test based on Wilson's work at least 50 items. An individual informal test can circumvent this difficulty in that it allows the tester to ask diagnostic questions. Interpreting information solely from written work is inevitably speculative.

Supporting tests could well include a simple test of short-term memory, for example, a digit span test, especially if a reverse digit span test is incorporated. Short-term memory is such a fundamental skill for mathematics, particularly, but not exclusively for mental arithmetic. For example, a 14-year-old pupil whose memory was around the three-item level analysed the sequence abcdeabcdeabcdeabc . . . as 'abc dea bcd eab'.

One of the most common characteristics of dyslexics is their great problem with the instant recall of basic facts, particularly the multiplication facts. This will have a great impact on their accuracy and speed of working and probably other areas as well, such as the ability to work with sequences of numbers. Not only do we need to know which facts they know, but also how they attempt to access the facts they cannot instantly recall, the strategies they use. Thus, the question is more than just knowing which facts are available by immediate recall, but what strategies, if any are used to obtain answers, for example, counting on in 5's for 7×5 or adding on one 8 to 5×8 (as 40) to work out that 6×8 is 48.

Anxiety and attitude can be critical issues, too. Simple questions such as 'Do you think you are any good at mathematics?' and 'Which bits of mathematics do you like best?' can provide useful information. There is a test for mathematics anxiety, the Mathematics Anxiety Rating Scale (Suinn 1972).

A diagnosis should show the interaction of many factors. Thinking style is one of the important learning factors where the impact is very dependent on other difficulties such as short-term memory.

THINKING STYLE: *INCHWORMS* AND *GRASSHOPPERS*

Two American high school teachers (Bath and Knox 1984) had noticed that some of their dyslexic students responded to Knox's teaching style and methods whilst others responded to Bath's. Analysis of the two teaching styles led to the development of the *'grasshopper'* and *'inchworm'* theory of thinking/cognitive styles in mathematics. The characteristics of the two styles are summarised in Table 2.1 (Chinn and Ashcroft 1998). The *Test of Thinking Style in Mathematics* (Chinn 2003) presents a subject with a series of maths questions each of which may be solved by an *inchworm* or a *grasshopper* method. The diagnosis of thinking style for each item starts with observing the subject's behaviour and the question 'How did you do that?' and possibly a follow-up question 'Can you think of another way to do that?' The answer to the question(s) is matched against described methods in the Manual to determine the thinking style for each question.

Here are two questions to illustrate the two styles, and some of the other influencing factors. These influencing factors illustrate the need to know 'What the child/learner brings to the problem'

Example 1:   A mental arithmetic problem

What is $340 - 97$?

An *inchworm* takes the numbers exactly as they are given and looks for a procedure to solve the problem. It is likely that he will visualise the question as if it were written as shown in Figure 2.1 and will solve it as a written problem including renaming 40 as 30 and 10, renaming 330 as 200 and 130. The answer will be computed from units (3) to tens (4) to hundreds (2) and given in the reverse order of hundreds, tens, units (243). Among the skills the learner has to bring to this method is a knowledge of basic subtraction facts, the concept or recall of the renaming procedure, the ability to visualise the problem in the vertical form, the memory to hold the answer to each step and then reverse the order to give the correct answer. If all this is there then the method will be successful, but even then it may be slow and the

Table 2.1 Cognitive styles of the *inchworm* and the *grasshopper*

	Inchworm	Grasshopper
First approach	1. Focusses on the parts and details 2. Looks at the numbers and facts to select a suitable formula or procedure	1. Overviews, holistic, puts together 2. Looks at the numbers and facts to estimate an answer, or narrow down the range of answers. Controlled exploration
Solving the problem	3. Formula, procedure oriented 4. Constrained focus. Uses one method 5. Works in serially ordered steps 6. Uses numbers exactly as given to make an easier calculation 7. More comfortable with paper and pen. Documents method	3. Answer oriented 4. Flexible focus. Uses a range of methods 5. Often works back from a trial answer usually forward 6. Adjusts, breaks down/builds up numbers 7. Rarely documents method. Performs calculations mentally (and intuitively)
Checking and evaluating	8. Unlikely to check or evaluate answer. If a check is done it will be by the same procedure/method 9. Often does not understand procedures or values of numbers. Works mechanically	8. Likely to appraise and evaluate answer against original estimate. Checks by an alternative method/procedure 9. Good understanding of number, methods and relationships

expectation is that mental arithmetic is done quickly, so when the correct answer is shouted out in class, the *inchworm* is likely to abandon ship and stop work.

A *grasshopper* is likely to overview the question, looking at both numbers (the *inchworm* may well stop at the − sign and enter subtraction mode). He will appraise the 97 and take it to 100, making the first stage of his

$$\begin{array}{r} \overset{2\ 13\ 10}{\cancel{3}\ \cancel{4}\ 0} \\ -\ 9\ 7 \\ \hline 2\ 4\ 3 \end{array}$$

Figure 2.1 An *inchworm* method of solving a problem

computation $340 - 100 = 240$. He then realises that the subtraction of 100 instead of 97 requires an adjustment and adds back 3. This method has made far less demands on memory, but requires an understanding of the values and inter-relationship of numbers. *Inchworms* do not easily see 100 as an alternative to 97. If they do subtract 100 then they are uncertain as to the compensatory addition (of 3).

Example 2:   A geometric/shape problem. The dog

> What is the area of the shaded part of Figure 2.2 (A written answer, with method is expected).

An *inchworm* with few mathematical skills may well simply count the squares. A more sophisticated inchworm will analyse the parts of the figure, seeing a triangle, a square and two thin rectangles. Then, if he brings a knowledge of area to the problem he may well calculate the area of the triangle from the formula $1/2 \times$ base $\times$ height and thus onto the square and the 'legs'

Head/triangle	area $= 1/2 \times 4 \times 4 = 8$	
Body/square	area $= 4 \times 4 = 16$	subtotal 24
leg 1	area $= 4$	subtotal 28
leg 2	area $= 4$	total 32

The addition of the area of each part is likely to be sequential and irrespective of any number bonds for ten, as in adding a leg to the body to make 20. *Inchworms* tend not to overview or, indeed look ahead.

On the positive side, the *inchworm* will be able to document his method, quote formulae and show that, even if he makes an error with the calculation, he has knowledge of area calculations.

The *grasshopper* may seek to redesign and simplify the problem. He will take a holistic view, trying to put the parts together, so the triangle is 'seen' as half of a 4×4 square. The gap between the two legs is also half of a 4×4

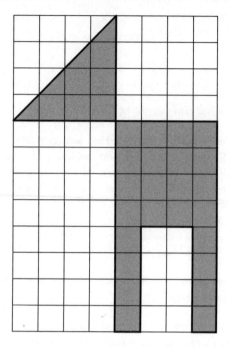

Figure 2.2 What is the area of the shaded part of the figure?

square, so the triangle can be used to fill that gap and make a 4 × 8 rectangle giving an area of 32. This method is far more difficult for the pupil to document.

In 1986, the author, working with Bath and Knox devised a *Test of Cognitive Style* (now out of print, see Chinn (2003)) based on this work. The test/re-test reliability data showed a continuum of styles from extreme *inchworm* to extreme *grasshopper*. Krutetskii (1976) wrote of the need for mathematicians to be flexible, to be 'harmonious' in their use of cognitive style. If one overlays the problems faced by dyslexic learners then the consequences of cognitive style are exacerbated.

So an *inchworm* with a poor working memory, a poor mathematical memory and poor sequential skills will be disadvantaged, especially in mental arithmetic tasks. An inaccurate, perhaps impetuous *grasshopper* will be severely disadvantaged in UK schools where the maths culture is based very firmly on documentation of methods. *Inchworms* also suffer from their tendency not to overview a problem.

The test/re-test results also showed that a learner may be *inchworm* in mental arithmetic and *grasshopper* in shape/geometric questions or vice versa. Cognitive style may well not be pervasive or habitual (in contrast with Riding and Rayner's (1998) statement that cognitive style is habitual).

In a recent classroom study (Chinn *et al.* 2001) working with children from England, Ireland and the Netherlands we found that the maths curriculum can have an impact on cognitive style. We also found that predictions of cognitive style have to consider all the factors and that the 'academic' factors may not always be the dominant influence.

The study looked at samples of 22 pupils in the 11–13 years age range, from three specialist schools and three mainstream schools in the three countries. The pupils were individually given 13 questions which were designed to diagnose cognitive style. After each item, they were asked to explain, 'How did you do that?' The methods were checked against known strategies and methods for each cognitive style. The results for the cohorts showed that, in the mainstream classes:

the Dutch pupils showed a slight dominance of *grasshopper* style
the English pupils showed an almost equal balance
the Irish pupils showed a striking preponderance of *inchworm* style.

As with all the results from the study, the cohort results often disguised individual anomalies, which would challenge an overly universal application of the findings to every child.

Our hypothesis for the Irish result was that the maths curriculum in place at that time (1999) was very prescriptive in the methods and algorithms that could be taught. The introduction of the new curricula has redressed the situation and encourages flexibility in methods.

The Dutch 'Realistic Maths' scheme encourages different styles for solving problems and the new National Numeracy Strategy (NNS) in the UK will also follow this fundamental principle. Indeed, there is evidence that this is a worldwide trend, taking in countries such as Japan and Hong Kong.

So our hypothesis then extends to suggesting that a teaching programme can impact on cognitive style and that schemes like the NNS or CAME (Cognitive Acceleration in Maths Education 2000) can have an influence on children's thinking style.

Then we analysed the results of the dyslexic pupils. If I ask the question during a lecture to a group of teachers, 'Which would you predict, dyslexic pupils are more inchworm or more grasshopper than the non-dyslexic pupils?' the majority vote is usually for the *grasshopper* style. But our results showed, quite dramatically, the opposite. In all three countries the dyslexic pupil cohort showed a greater proportion of *inchworm* thinking style.

Our hypothesis for this result is that, as with the 'no answer' error, the dyslexic pupils are taking the safer route and using what has been taught, usually as the generic method, irrespective of its suitability to them.

In the first edition of this book I wrote of the interaction of teachers' cognitive style with pupils' cognitive style. Again in the many lectures I have given on cognitive style to teachers in many countries, a straw poll of the preferred cognitive style shows a split that rarely goes beyond 40–60 (percentage), either way. Obviously yet another reason why some children say they learn better with one teacher than another.

There are a number of researchers who have written about cognitive style and thinking style in mathematics. For example, Skemp (1986) called the two style 'instrumental' and 'relational', Harvey (1982) calls the two styles 'geometers' and 'algebraists'. Marolda and Davidson (2000) describe Learning Styles I and II and Sharma (1989) writes about 'qualitative' learning personalities and 'quantitative' learning personalities, broadening the construct beyond just cognition.

Extending the concept beyond just mathematics, de Bono describes 'lateral' and 'vertical' styles of thinking. The following passage is worth quoting in full: 'Lateral thinking is quite distinct from vertical thinking, which is the traditional type of thinking. In vertical thinking one moves forward by sequential steps, each of which must be justified. . . . In lateral thinking one may have to be wrong at some stage in order to obtain a correct solution. Lateral thinking does not exclude other pathways. Both types of thinking are required. They are complementary' (de Bono 1970).

de Bono's words are reinforcing the need to encourage both styles (Krutetskii's 'harmonious' thinking) but he also explains that the lateral thinker has to accept that he may be wrong at some stage in order to move to a correct answer. This implies that the lateral thinker has to take a risk and be comfortable with being wrong on the way to being right. There are implications here for the dyslexic learner.

Consequences for pupils

I have already hinted at several implications of cognitive style for the dyslexic learner. In the early part of the chapter, I spoke of knowing what the child brings to the problem, his knowledge of maths, his attitudes and attributes, and then his cognitive/thinking style. It is the different interactions of the many influencing facts and the task that makes diagnosis a fascinating and eclectic activity.

One of the reinforcing reasons for using *grasshopper* strategies will be a limited ability to recall basic facts rapidly. If the child develops strategies (Ackerman *et al.* 1986) then the interaction of a *grasshopper* style and strategies which circumvent problems with the recall of basic facts will be mutually supportive. However, the documentation of these strategies is likely to be less sequentially logical and often more difficult to explain than a more formula-based method. Because a *grasshopper* relates harder numbers to easier numbers, for example, 97 to 100, he is often better at estimations or questions where the best strategy is to throw in a number and use trial and adjust. *Grasshoppers* are not method oriented, at least not in terms of exclusive methods, but are answer oriented.

An example of this will be their reaction to early algebra, where they are being taught to solve an equation such as

$$y + 5 = 11$$

by learning the procedure, for example, subtracting 5 from each side. Their initial response is to see the answer is 6 and then be completely uninvolved in the procedure. Of course, in later examples which are more challenging, the procedure will be necessary.

Grasshoppers who lose accuracy perhaps due to an impetuous attitude will almost certainly fail. There is no method to explain their thinking and the answer is wrong.

An *inchworm* with good recall of basic facts and good short- and long-term memories is unlikely to be an inspired problem solver, but will probably have few difficulties in surviving mathematics. They may well use the approach of not wishing to actually understand the formula, but just be able to remember it and apply it. The *inchworm* is very formula/procedure oriented.

But if the *inchworm* does not have good recall of basic facts and formulae, then he is a great risk. The use of compensating strategies which rely on inter-relating numbers is going to be less attractive and take much longer to internalise. Since many dyslexics have poor recall of basic facts (Miles 1993) and poor short-term memories (Miles 1993) then they are less likely to be successful *inchworms*, yet our survey suggests that they may perceive this as their best option. One might also assume that although precision teaching may be the most effective approach, progress will be slow and require much revision and overlearning.

Generally speaking, the learner needs to master the basic skills of both thinking styles. For example, the *grasshopper* needs to learn how to analyse his thinking and document it. The *inchworm* needs to learn how to overview and pre-estimate answers. Experience suggests that there will be some learners for whom style is habitual. In these cases the teacher needs to be aware of this and acknowledge it and help the pupil make the best of his restricted thinking style. As ever, there should be a balance of pushing for change and recognising when this is counter-productive.

Teaching to both cognitive styles

Despite the warning in the sentence in the previous section, it seems incumbent upon teachers to teach flexibility for thinking through and solving maths problems. To illustrate how one can teach to both styles I have chosen two topics. The first relates to learning times tables facts.

Amazingly, often I hear people talk about learning times tables in this sort of fashion, 'Well, I had to learn them when I was a child. We just chanted them until we learnt them. It never hurt me to have to learn them'.

Most children can learn or access some of these elusive facts, usually the $2\times$, $5\times$ and $10\times$ (and, of course the $0\times$ and $1\times$). Here the patterns are relatively simple. Devlin (2000) contrasts people's problems with learning, what are in effect only 18 facts (that are left when the easier ones are mastered) with a typical vocabulary at 6 of around 20,000 words.

The UK's NNS does expect children to learn these facts, but it also acknowledges that they may use strategies to work out unknown facts such as $4\times$ from known facts such as $2\times$ (twice). The 1999 maths curriculum for Ireland actually states that pupils may benefit from using the easy facts to work out the harder facts. It seems to me that we have to acknowledge that rote learning these facts is not a realistic possibility for some learners. Dehaene (1997) speculates as to reasons why the task is so hard, citing linguistic confusions, but our recent studies suggest that this does not cover all the possibilities. When it comes to maths errors, pupils are creative.

An *inchworm* may benefit from using self-voice echo (Lane and Chinn 1986) where rote learning makes use of the child's own voice. An *inchworm* may well appreciate the (gypsy) finger method for the $9\times$ facts (Chinn 1996), but neither of these methods will work for all children or adults.

If maths facts are taught and learnt as separate facts, without patterns and inter-relationships, then the task is huge. There are also dangers, for example a child may not see the multiplication facts as also being division facts. The hardest fact $8 \times 7 = 56$ can illustrate this. It is one of two facts from the table facts that follows a number sequence 5678, that is $56 = 7 \times 8$. It is not unusual for pupils to react to this revelation by saying, 'Ha, but that's not $7 \times 8 = 56$'. The reversal of the numbers compared to the familiar sequence devalues the aid.

Many children use strategies to access facts. A common example is to use doubles plus or minus 1 as in $8 + 7$ as 2×8 minus 1. A less frequent example came from a 15-year-old boy making use of a fact learnt as a speech therapy exercise. He had learnt 'Six sixes are thirty six' which is challenging verbally. He then used this fact to work out 3×6, by halving 36.

Perhaps we maths teachers could spend a little more time teaching children (and adults) to use the 'easy' numbers to work out the 'hard' numbers. We manage with our coins, using only 1p, 2p, 5p, 10p, 20p, 50p, £1, £2, £5 and so on.

So, a logical strategy for deriving $4 \times$ facts is to double the doubles, a process that can be reversed for dividing by 4. A strategy may be implemented totally by a pupil or may just increase the number of accessible facts. So in this strategy for $4 \times$, 4×6 and 4×7 are relatively easy double doubles. 4×8 requires the pupil to double 16, which can be seen as $2(15 + 1)$. Most of the strategies involve two easier steps rather than one difficult or impossible step.

The strategy of multiplying by 2×2 instead of 4 is, of course the same principle as multiplying by 2×10 instead of 20, for example.

Learning to calculate the $9 \times$ facts by starting with $10 \times$ facts and adjusting back teaches several skills, including estimation, refining an estimation and patterns. The pattern for the computation is that a number times nine is equal to the number times 10 minus the number. For example 7×9 starts with 7×10 (70) and then subtracts 7 to give 63. Another pattern for nines is that the digits in the answer will add to make 9, in this case $6 + 3$. So the *inchworm* is learning an estimation skill, being shown patterns, whilst the *grasshopper* is organising his skills and strategies.

For the $3 \times$, $6 \times$ and $7 \times$ facts, the strategy used is based on multiplication as repeated addition, but not one by one additions as an *inchworm* may try, but chunked additions. So the $4 \times$ facts are computed from 4 as 2×2. The $3 \times$ facts can be computed as $2 \times$ plus $1 \times$, the $6 \times$ facts as $5 \times$ plus $1 \times$ and the $7 \times$ as $5 \times$ plus $2 \times$.

> Thus 3×6 is accessed as $2 \times 6 = 12$ and then $12 + 6 = 18$.
> This can be visualised as $6 + 6 + 6$, with two 6's grouped.
> 6×8 is done in two steps as $5 \times 8 = 40$ and then $40 + 8 = 48$.
> This can be visualised as $8 + 8 + 8 + 8 + 8 + 8$, with five 8's grouped.
> 7×7 begins with $5 \times 7 = 35$ and then adds on 14 from 2×7 to make 49.
> This can be visualised as $7 + 7 + 7 + 7 + 7 + 7 + 7$, with five 7's grouped and two 7's grouped (see Figure 2.3).

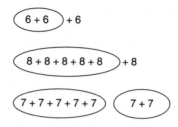

Figure 2.3 Chunking in order to add

It should be noted that some children may not be able to instantly recall the 2× facts, but will finger count in twos to obtain their answer. Once again patterns can be used to support memory and learning. The 2 4 6 8 0 sequence recurs throughout the doubles. As far as the 2× table facts are concerned, that is 1 × 2 to 10 × 2, 5 × 2 acts as a half way marker. Our fingers give the answer as 10. Subsequent facts are 6 (5 + 1), 7 (5 + 2), 8 (5 + 3) and 9 (10 − 1) or in this special case (5 + 4). So, using 8 × 2 as an example, since 8 is 5 and 3, the 5 × 2 gives 10 (one of the easiest of the easy facts) and the 3 × 2 gives 6 to make the answer 16. All the learner really needs is 2 × 3 = 6 as the 10 is already there for all the 6 × 2 to 9 × 2 facts.

For the *inchworm* there is an opportunity to learn some *grasshopper* skills. For the *grasshopper* there is the opportunity to rationalise and unify his strategies. Both styles are learning to generalise, use patterns, inter-relate numbers and the operations and thus link back to established facts. Strategies take a task which is impossible for many dyslexics and reduce the problem, hopefully to a manageable level.

For a second example I have chosen a selection of basic numeracy questions (taken from Foundation level GCSE work). In each example use is made of key facts, such as the number bonds for 10 and an interchange of operations, such as rewording a division question to make it a multiplication question.

Q1. Dan wants to share his bingo winnings of £96 between his six grandchildren. How much does each child get?

'Share' would suggest that the operation to use is division. This would lead to 96 ÷ 6 and to many dyslexics not attempting the question. If the student thinks of the six grandchildren getting £*y*, then 6*y* must equal 96 (though this reasoning may not be visualised as algebra!).

So, if each child receives £10, then 6 × £10 = £60.

There is some way to go to reach £90, so more money is needed. 6 × £5 is half of 6 × £10, so £30, taking the total to £90.

Simple observation shows a further $6 \times £1$ takes the total to £96, giving each child $£10 + 5 + 1 = £16$.

An *inchworm* with knowledge of the 6 times facts will perform a short division. He will be less likely to appraise the answer or check by multiplying 6×16.

Q2. A box of fudge is labelled 1.6 kg.

Here is a rough rule for converting kilograms to pounds

Kilograms $\times 2.2 =$ Pounds

Use this rule to convert 1.6 kg to pounds.

An *inchworm* will set up a long multiplication

$$
\begin{array}{r}
1.6 \\
\times 2.2 \\
\hline
3.2 \\
.32 \\
\hline
3.52
\end{array}
$$

A *grasshopper* will see that to multiply by 2.2 you double and add one-tenth of the double (0.2 is one-tenth of 2) so the calculation becomes

3.2 plus 0.32 which is 3.52 pounds

Q3. Sam asked 13 people how many kilometres they travelled to work. Here are their answers

6   11   5   10   7   9   8   23   9   6   5   11   7

What is the average distance travelled?

A *grasshopper* will add by pairing and grouping

$$
\begin{array}{rcl}
9 + 11 &=& 20 \\
9 + 11 &=& 20 \\
5 + 5 + 10 &=& 20 \\
7 + 7 + 6 &=& 20 \\
23 + 8 &=& 31 \\
6 &=& \underline{6} \\
& & 117
\end{array}
$$

using $13 \times 10 = 130$, the answer must be 9.

The *grasshopper* is using key numbers and flexible use of the operations, once again interchanging division and multiplication.

The *inchworm* will add the thirteen numbers, in the order they are given and try to divide the total by 13. He may well decide that the second step is beyond him and stop. He is less likely to see that 117 is close to 10 × 13.

Cognitive style and the NNS

I have already introduced the matter of curriculum design and content influencing pupils' cognitive style. To take the issue further I have looked at the requirements the English NNS asks of its pupils as an example of the interaction of curricula expectations and children's cognitive style. As one might hope, the expectation is for flexibility in thinking styles.

Where a requirement is *inchworm* I have used italics, where the requirement is **grasshopper** I have used bold. Where it is not clear which is the preferred thinking style I have used plain text.

The NNS states your pupils should

- **Have the sense of the size of a number and where it fits in the number system.**
- *Know by heart number facts, such as number bonds* (10) *multiplication tables*, **doubles and halves.**
- **Use what they know by heart to figure out answers mentally.**
- Calculate accurately and efficiently, both **mentally** and *with paper and pencil*, **drawing on a range of calculation strategies.**
- Recognise when it is appropriate to use a calculator and be able to do so effectively.
- **Make sense of number problems, including non-routine problems,** *and recognise the operations needed to solve them.*
- *Explain their methods and reasoning using correct mathematical terms.*
- **Judge whether their answers are reasonable and have strategies for checking them where necessary.**

All of this will have interactions and overlays with other learning factors, such as memory and speed of working, but it does illustrate how one particular construct has significant consequences for learners. Roughly speaking the outcomes split half and half, so if a learner is at either end of the thinking/cognitive style continuum, then he will experience difficulties with half of the curriculum.

CONCLUSION

The concept of different thinking/cognitive styles, though relevant in the case of all pupils, is particularly relevant in the teaching of dyslexics. The diagnosis and subsequent intervention programme offered, and even the mainstream programme, should acknowledge that not all children process numbers in the same way and that children have different and individual combinations of skills and knowledge. The typical dyslexic problems of difficulties with rote learning, short-term memory deficits and weaknesses in arranging symbolic material in sequence are likely to make many standard mathematical methods and basic facts difficult to learn.

The dyslexic in this position will either start to develop his own strategies, which may not be systematic, efficient or organised, or may give up on mathematics altogether. The advantage of the *inchworm/grasshopper* concept is that if it is introduced in classrooms (and this is to a large extent true in the new NNS in England) then all pupils will benefit from the greater flexibility in using numbers. They will have a better chance of experiencing success and a wider set of learning experiences from which to develop concepts. The thought of dividing classes up into *inchworms* and *grasshoppers*, and intermediates (*grassworms* or *inchhoppers*) is bizarre. Instead a flexible programme will address both styles and be appropriate for a wide range of children. It will be fascinating to see what this aspect of the NNS achieves for all pupils, but especially dyslexic pupils.

REFERENCES

Ackerman, P.T., Anhalt, J.M. and Dykman, R.A. (1986) 'Arithmetic automatisation failure in children with attention and reading disorders: associations and sequela', *Journal of Learning Disabilities*, 19(4), 222–32.

Ashlock, R.B. (1994) *Error Patterns in Computation* (6th edn), Englewood Cliffs, NJ, Prentice Hall.

Ashlock, R.B. (1998) *Error Patterns in Computation* (7th edn), Upper Saddle River, NJ, Simon and Schuster.

Bath, J.B. and Knox, D.E. (1984) 'Two styles of performing maths', in J.B. Bath, S.J. Chinn and D.E. Knox (eds) *Dyslexia: Research and its Application to the Adolescent*, Bath, Better Books.

Borasi, R. (1985) 'Using errors as springboards for the learning of mathematics: an introduction', *Focus on Learning Problems in Mathematics*, 7(34), 1–15.

CAME (2000) *Cognitive Acceleration in Mathematics Education*, London, Department of Education and Professional Studies, Kings College.

Chinn, S.J. (1995) 'A pilot study to compare aspects of arithmetic skills', *Dyslexia Review*, 4, 4–7.

Chinn, S. (1996) *What to do When you can't Learn the Times Tables*, Baldock, Egon.

Chinn, S.J. (2003) *Test of Thinking Style in Mathematics*, Belford, Ann Arbor.

Chinn, S.J. and Ashcroft, J.R. (1998) *Mathematics for Dyslexics: A Teaching Handbook* (2nd edn), London, Whurr.

Chinn, S., McDonagh, D., Van Elswijk, R., Harmsen, H., Kay, J., McPhillips, T., Power, A. and Skidmore, L. (2001) 'Classroom studies into cognitive style in mathematics for pupils with dyslexia in special education in the Netherlands, Ireland and the UK', *British Journal of Special Education*, 28(2), 80–4.

Clausen-May, T., Clatdon, H. and Ruddock, G. (2000) *Numeracy Impact*, Windsor, NFER-Nelson.

de Bono, E. (1970) *Lateral Thinking: A Textbook of Creativity*, London, Ward Lock Educational.

Dehaene, S. (1997) *The Number Sense: How the Mind Creates Mathematics*, New York, Oxford University Press.

Devlin, K. (2000) *The Maths Gene*, London, Weidenfeld and Nicolson.

DfEE (1999) *The National Numeracy Strategy. Framework for Teaching Mathematics from Reception to Year 6*, London, Department for Education and Employment, London.

France, N. (1979) *The Profile of Mathematical Skills*, Windsor, NFER-Nelson.

Harvey, R. (1982) 'I can keep going if I want to: one way of looking at learning mathematics', in R. Harvey, D. Kerslake, H. Shuard and M. Torbe (eds) *Language Teaching and Learning. 6. Mathematics*, London, Ward Lock Educational.

Jastak, S.J. and Jastak, G.S. (1993) *Wide Range Achievement Test*, Wilmington, DE, Jastak Associates.

Kaufman, A. (2002) 'Policy on dyslexia', Lecture at the Uppsala Conference.

Krutetskii, V.A. (1976) in J. Kilpatrick and I. Wirszup (eds) *The Psychology of Mathematical Abilities in School Childern*, Chicago, University of Chicago Press.

Lane, C. and Chinn, S.J. (1986) 'Learning by self-voice echo', *Academic Therapy*, 21, 477–81.

Marolda, M.R. and Davidson, P.S. (2000) 'Mathematical Learning Profiles and Differentiated Teaching Strategies', *Perspectives*, 26(3), 10–15.

Miles, T.R. (1993) *Dyslexia: The Pattern of Difficulties* (2nd edn), London, Whurr.

Riding, R.J. and Rayner, S. (1998) *Cognitive Styles and Learning Strategies*, London, David Fulton.

Rust, J. (1996) *Weschler Objectives Numerical Dimensions*, London, The Psychological Corporation.

Sharma, M.C. (1989) 'Mathematics learning personality', *Math Notebook*, 7(1,2).

Skemp, R.R. (1986) *The Psychology of Learning Mathematics* (2nd edn), Harmondsworth, Pelican.

Suinn, R. (1972) *Mathematics Anxiety Rating Scale*, RMBSI Colorado.

Vernon, P.E., Miller, K.M. and Izard, J.F. (1995) *Mathematics Competency Test*, London, Hodder and Stoughton.

Vincent, D. and Crumpler, M. (2000) *Numeracy Progress Tests*, London, Hodder and Stoughton.

Wilson, J. and Sadowski, B. (eds) (1976) *The Maryland Diagnostic Test and Interview Protocols*, University of Maryland Arithmetic Centre.

Chapter 3

Linking language to action

Mary Kibel

A LESSON WITH ALEX

Some years ago, I took an Open University course on teaching mathematics. It was called 'Developing Mathematical Thinking'. As part of the course we had to try various activities with a child and notice his approach. I worked with a dyslexic 14-year-old called Alex. One of the activities we were asked to try was a game called 'Shrink-A-Square'. It had been designed to teach decomposition – the 'borrowing' procedure in subtraction. This game had such a surprising effect on Alex, that I shall describe it here in detail.

We played with Dienes blocks[1] on boards marked in columns with 'hundreds', 'tens' and 'units'. We each started off with a block of 100 which we placed in the hundreds-position on our boards. This was the square that we had to 'shrink'. Then we threw a dice in turn and took away the number we threw. If the subtraction involved decomposition, we had to exchange one large block for ten smaller ones before we could take away. The winner was the first person to end up with no blocks at all.

This was simple enough – but the manipulation of the blocks had to be accompanied by a verbal description of what was happening. If the subtraction involved exchange, we had to accompany the operation with a precise mathematical statement to describe what we were doing – 'I take one ten from the tens-position and exchange it for ten units. I put the ten units in the units-position, and then I take away the six.' The aim of the activity was to encourage children to practise and perfect the language of exchange.

Alex and I took a long time working our way down from 100. It became much too easy, and so to make the game more fun we began closing our eyes as we manipulated the blocks and described what we were doing. Next, we tried describing the whole process, eyes shut, without touching the blocks at all. This proved surprisingly hard for Alex. He seemed to find it extremely difficult to sustain the language on its own, and the temptation to open his eyes and handle the blocks was very strong. But eventually, given time and practice, the verbal explanation became easy and the blocks almost superfluous. At this point we transferred to the formal written algorithm. The transition was swift and trouble-free, and Alex left that afternoon feeling that we had had an amusing time, nothing more.

However, the effect was dramatic. Alex was 14. He had never understood how to do subtraction when this involved 'borrowing'. He regularly took the lowest numbers from the highest, regardless of whether they were on the top or bottom line – and he regularly got his answers wrong! Some time later, he called round and proudly announced, 'I can do those take-aways. They're easy. We've been doing them at school this week and I got the whole lot right. No problem! They're *ace*, they are.'

I was surprised. I gave him a few to do, and sure enough, he worked his way through them faultlessly with great ease and enjoyment. A month later he could still do them and to my knowledge he has not forgotten to this day.

SOME GUIDING PRINCIPLES

I was puzzled by what had happened. Nine years of careful schooling had not taught Alex how to subtract when this involved exchange, and yet the half-hour spent on this simple game had succeeded in getting the concept across in a secure and permanent way. What did the 'Shrink-A-Square' game offer that normal teaching lacked?

Alex was dyslexic – it was possible that certain aspects of the game were particularly relevant to dyslexia and that this was the reason for its success. I felt that this was worth pursuing and analysed the activity more carefully.

One striking feature was that at no point did I have to *tell* Alex what to do. As he worked with the blocks, the procedure for decomposition was obvious and so no verbal explanation was necessary.

Dyslexics have difficulty with language. If mathematics is taught through the medium of language, if children are told what to do and expected to remember a sequence of verbal instructions, then dyslexic children are going to find this hard. We are asking them to rely on an area in which we know they are cognitively weak.

When we translate the procedure into a visual form that can be manipulated and solved spatially, there is an important change of emphasis. We engage non-verbal routes to understanding and reduce the role of language. For a dyslexic, this change of approach could be a particularly helpful one.

Yet the 'Shrink-A-Square' game did not reduce the role of language completely. Rather the reverse – the language and manipulating seemed to work together in a mutually supportive way. Each time Alex went through the procedure for decomposition, he had to describe what he was doing in words. The language reinforced the sequence of actions. This is verbal labelling. It is a strategy that most people use to help them remember things.

We know that dyslexics are poor at verbal labelling. When Alex played the 'Shrink-A-Square' game, he was forced to use this strategy in a very precise and deliberate way. The effect of this could have been to strengthen an area in which he is naturally weak – and this may have helped him remember the sequence of operations needed for the complicated 'borrowing' procedure.

Moreover, there was considerable overlearning of the language. During our half-hour session we played several games and Alex must have repeated the language of exchange some 20 to 30 times! But what is more interesting – the talking ran alongside the manipulating. We were 'tying' the language to visual and kinesthetic images. Alex talked as he handled as he looked. It was multisensory learning.

Dyslexics have difficulty with mathematical terms. The words do not hold meaning easily. For Alex the terms 'exchange', 'tens-position', 'one ten for ten units' became bound to the action. Later, if meaning fades, the words themselves should conjure up clear kinesthetic and visual images of what we were doing. This means that, as well as practising the mathematical language, we were giving it meaning and solidity. We were helping to make it permanent. And we did so in a multisensory way.

These ideas have now become the basis of all the work I do with dyslexic children. When I teach mathematics, I try to structure each learning situation in a very deliberate way.

If I teach something new, I never ask children to rely on a sequence of verbal instructions – I never *tell* them what to do. Instead I create a physical representation of the concept and give them problems to solve by manipulation. This increases opportunities for non-verbal learning and reduces dependence on language.

I strengthen the role of verbal labelling by arranging for language to run alongside the manipulating. I try to make this a prominent and challenging part of the activity by insisting that the language is precise and allowing no short cuts!

Strong kinesthetic and visual images should underlie mathematical terms. I always arrange for considerable overlearning of the language, and ensure that abstract terms are linked to a concrete base.

None of this is new, of course. Teachers have always maintained that children learn best by doing, particularly in the early years. The main thrust of the course 'Developing Mathematical Thinking' was precisely this. Concepts should not be passed on ready-made. They should be allowed to grow in concrete situations and only later should formal written work take place.

What I have tried to show is that this approach has very clear advantages for dyslexics. It gives solid support in areas where language is weak. For children like Alex who repeatedly forget despite years of careful teaching this may be a safer way in which to learn.

ALLOWING TIME FOR CONCEPTS TO FORM

In a moment I shall give examples of how these ideas work out in practice, but before I do so, I would like to look more closely at an important aspect of the 'Shrink-A-Square' game – the concrete nature of the learning and the length of time that it took.

Alex and I spent a full half-hour on the 'Shrink-A-Square' game and during that time the learning passed through several interesting stages.

At first the language itself was difficult – the words were unfamiliar, and the length and precision of the statement awkward to cope with. As fluency developed, Alex began to talk his way through the procedure with confidence. Yet for a long time the language remained curiously dependent on the action. He could not hold the idea in his head. When he tried to describe the process with his eyes closed, he faltered and the description became muddled and confused. The need to handle the blocks and look at the visual layout was very great indeed. Alex seemed to understand quite clearly what he was doing, but the understanding was embedded[2] in the concrete situation. The concept could not stand alone.

Eventually, of course, the need for tangible support did fall away. Handling the blocks became unnecessary and almost annoying. Alex could explain the whole procedure, eyes shut, with no difficulty at all. This was the point at which he mastered the process. An internal model had formed. The 'Shrink-A-Square' game had done its work.

It was then that we changed to normal written subtraction. Alex found this easy to do. Even an unexpected nought on the top line presented no problem. Alex could 'see' that one hundred needed to be exchanged for 10 tens. He could dip down into more concrete levels of thinking. His newly won concept was functioning well. It had evolved slowly in a concrete situation and was very solidly underpinned. But it had taken a surprisingly long time.

Perhaps the most helpful thing about the 'Shrink-A-Square' game was that, by chance, it held Alex in a concrete learning situation for an unusual length of time. It was long enough for the whole process of concept formation to be fully complete by the time he came to tackle formal subtraction. The result of this was that Alex did not have to remember a set of rules, and when he met an unexpected problem – the nought on the top line – he did not need to ask me what to do. He was able to work things out for himself by drawing on his sound underlying knowledge of the full procedure for subtraction.

Perhaps the reason for his sudden competence was that he no longer needed to remember a sequence of verbal instructions. He could work directly from a basic understanding of the process, and when the need arose he was able to translate back to more concrete ways of thinking.

Many dyslexic youngsters do become quite good at mathematics. They too seem to work in this way, often solving problems by unconventional methods because they prefer to work from the underlying concept, the *sense* in the situation, rather than by following the teacher's rule. Perhaps these children have discovered for themselves that they can avoid their linguistic limitation by working in more direct and concrete ways.

Another factor may be involved here. It is possible that, because of a generalized weakness in language, dyslexics have difficulty with the process of concept formation itself. Their thinking may remain embedded in concrete situations for longer than is usual with other children. The jump from concrete to abstract may happen less easily for them. In the 'Shrink-A-Square' game, Alex spent a very long lime at the manipulating stage of the learning. It was far longer than I would have thought necessary. Yet this may have provided him, by chance, with just the opportunity he needed.

So my final guiding principle is this. Arrange for children to develop their thinking in concrete situations but, above all, allow them plenty of time for this. Half-formed concepts are elusive – they still require verbal support and are easily forgotten. Dyslexic children need to be able *to complete* their learning with concrete materials and we have to create the opportunities for them to do so.

SOME TEACHING EXAMPLES

I have found these basic ideas extremely useful, especially for children who puzzle us because they persistently forget despite years of careful teaching and every opportunity to learn.

I would like to illustrate them with examples of things that work for me. Most of the children I describe attend our dyslexia workshop on a Saturday. We work chiefly on reading and spelling, and tackle mathematics only if children are having persistent difficulty at school.

I usually work with parent and child together. I devise the concrete learning situation beforehand and decide on the language to accompany it. We develop this in the lesson and once it is going smoothly the parent takes over. If everything goes well, they take the kit of materials home and practise during the week. The language is always carefully written down and they both agree to keep to it. This allows a great deal of unhurried talking and manipulating to take place and provides the *time* that children need.

In school, learning situations can be devised in which children work in pairs. The 'Shrink-A-Square' game was designed with this in mind. The teacher sets up the activity, develops the language and then leaves the children to continue on their own.

Once the concept is fully established, it is followed by formal written practice in the usual way. From time to time, I ask children to 'talk their way through' an operation or to explain why a particular step is necessary. This keeps alive the original language and understanding, and maintains links with the concrete stage of the learning.

Teaching addition with carrying to Gemma

My first example is Gemma, and the way she mastered the idea of 'carrying' in addition. Gemma worked on a large plastic-covered board marked in 'tens' and 'units' columns (Figure 3.1), and wrote on it with a black wipe-off pen. Under the line where the 'carried tens' are written was a picture of a little dog saying 'Wait here!' (see next page).

Gemma set out an addition sum with Dienes blocks and then I asked:

> 'How many tens have you in the tens position?'
> 'Two.' Gemma pointed to them.
> 'Write it down.' She wrote '2' next to the two rods.
> 'How many units have you in the units position?'
> 'Seven.' Gemma wrote '7' next to the seven units, and we dealt with each number in this way.

There was no explanation as such, but Gemma was developing a feel for the fact that '2' written in the tens-position meant two tens, and that '7' in the units-position meant seven units. She was able to *see* the Dienes blocks and figures juxtaposed, repeatedly, through countless exercises, and was strengthening her grasp of the place system.

Gemma had already done some addition using straws. She was used to putting an elastic band around ten straws to make 'one bundle' and moving it across to the tens-position. So in this game, when the units came to more

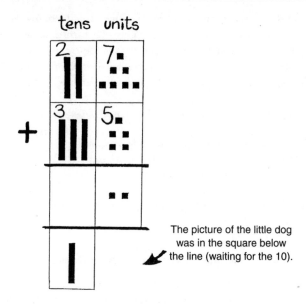

tens units

The picture of the little dog
was in the square below
the line (waiting for the 10).

Figure 3.1 Addition with carrying

than nine, she 'exchanged 10 units for one ten', and I said: 'Look, the little dog says "Wait here!"'.

Wait here!

She put the 'ten' under the line in the square with the little dog, and there it remained while she added up the rest of her tens. I gave no explanation for this, but made sure we joked continually about the little dog wanting the 'ten' to wait with him. And as he looked up appealingly from the bottom of the page, I could feel him making his point in Gemma's mind!

The transfer to the formal algorithm was smooth and required no further explanation. Gemma always put the figure she carried under the line, working confidently from the understanding she had gained from the manipulating stage of the learning. She always carried the correct figure, having mentally exchanged her units, and she always remembered where it had to 'wait'.

The language we carefully practised and overlearned was this:

> 'How many tens have you in the tens-position?'
> 'How many units have you in the units-position?'
> 'I need to exchange 10 units for one ten.'

The little dog was used to strengthen a feel for position without needing to explain things in words.

Multiplication – teaching the initial concept to Daniel

To beginners, the language used in multiplication can be confusing. If we say 'three threes are nine', the second 'three' means '3', but the first means something quite different – it means '3 lots of'.

To introduce this idea in a direct non-verbal way, I played a game with bright multicoloured map-pins on a cork floor-tile. I tipped a heap of pins on the table, and while they were still rolling around we each picked up three of the same colour and put them in a row on our cork boards. Then we made another row in a different colour. As we worked away, building up our boards, I developed the language along these lines:

> 'How many lots of three have you made, Daniel?'
> 'How many pink lots?'
> 'How many green lots?'
> 'Let's make another blue lot' – and so on.

When we had filled the boards, we played a game called 'STOP-ME'. I said, 'Daniel, stop me when I've counted *four* lots of three', and slowly counted the rows of pins.

> 'One, two, three . . . four, five, six . . . '

Daniel had to shout 'Stop!' as soon as I reached 12 but before I had time to sneak quickly on to 13. I counted rhythmically, quietly stressing 3, 6, 9, 12, and Daniel followed with his finger ready to shout 'Stop!' at just the right moment. To do this, he had to judge what '4 lots of 3' meant on his board and follow carefully while I counted. As he did so, he could *see* the 'lots of 3' as we built up the pattern. He was developing a feel for multiplication in his own way, without any explanation from me.

When this became easy, we swapped roles and Daniel did the counting. We counted quickly now, slightly emphasizing the key numbers at the end of each line. The 3× table was beginning to form. The words were tied to the rows of coloured pins and the number sequence was developing in a concrete situation.

Once 'lots of' was fixed, I alternated it with 'three threes' and finally introduced the more formal language and the symbol. For a long time Daniel used his map-pin board for calculations which required the 3× table, and for a long time the words 'lots of' were regularly alternated with the symbol '×' on my workcards. Gradually, the number sequence became internalized and he was able to work on his own, but whenever he got stuck he still went back to his well-worn board and counted the rows of pins.

By getting Daniel to use his map-pins over a very long period of time, I was able to ensure that the concept of multiplication was formed from a strong concrete base.

Long multiplication and division – with Kathy

Kathy is a bright and cheerful 13-year-old. 'If you can teach Kathy to multiply', her father said, 'I'll be very surprised. All her teachers have tried!'

Kathy could not multiply if it meant going beyond her table square:

'2 × 13? I haven't a *clue!*'
'Division? Oh, that's *IMPOSSIBLE!!*'

Kathy's difficulty was not the concepts. She understood exactly what was needed. It was remembering the sequence of operations in the complicated formal procedures that was 'impossible'.

The breakthrough came when we worked with large figures written on cards which were physically moved around and discussed. We worked on a large piece of white formica and scribbled and drew arrows with black dry-wipe pens. Kathy made overlapping cards like this:

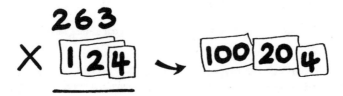

The numbers could be taken apart in layers as she multiplied by each one in turn, and then reassembled at the end as she explained to me why the final addition was necessary.

In division, we worked on a similar scale, but with piles of Dienes blocks instead of numbers. The remainders were 'exchanged' (with appropriate language) for ten smaller blocks, and the whole procedure accompanied by a lively flow of verbal labelling.

Dyslexics have difficulty with sequencing. In mathematics, the algorithms are often long sequences of fairly meaningless operations, and these usually have to be memorized *in words*. Children forget. They mix operations. They often resort to rows of tiny dots and tally marks in an attempt to find a way around the difficulty.

By working in this large multisensory way and developing an understanding of each process, Kathy was able to master these two complex algorithms so that they eventually became easy and fluent. If she forgets, she can draw on her kinesthetic and visual memory of what she did, as well as her knowledge of why each step is necessary. The need to rely on a sequence of verbal instructions has been reduced.

Division – teaching the initial concept to Robert

I was introducing the concept of division to Robert who is 11. His tables book was a mystery to him and he needed the concrete experience of division before we could begin. Young children will happily 'share' sweets among their Teddies and develop understanding in this way. With older children it is difficult. We tried 'sharing' beans in saucers, but this idea was too weak to grip his attention and it did not work.

The answer was to raise the level of difficulty so that it became a challenge and involved his full powers of concentration. I gave him a bag containing 25 wooden blocks and asked him to take out 12 and put them on the table in a row. Once Robert had set them up, he was not allowed to touch them. I asked him whether, just by looking at the blocks, he could divide them into 'lots of three'.

He stared at them for a while, visually dividing them into groups, concentrating hard so that he wouldn't lose his place:

> 'Yes! It's 4 lots of 3. Exactly!' he said, with a note of triumph in his voice.

We continued, Robert taking from the bag larger and larger handfuls of blocks as he felt he could cope with the challenge. He moved to more difficult tasks. There were 15 blocks set out on the table and I asked,

> 'How many 4's are there, and what's left over?'
> 'How many other ways can you divide them?'

Robert was not allowed to touch – however large the number of blocks. He gripped the edge of the table and his hands had to stay there! A fusion of number language and its concrete counterpart was there, and the level of concentration was high. Robert not only grasped the idea of division and remainder but internalized a useful range of number facts as well.

Later, he achieved significant moments like this. There were 18 blocks lined up on the table. Robert studied them carefully and announced:

> '6 lots of 3 . . .' long pause '. . . 9 lots of 2'

Then he hesitated, looked excited, thought around in his mind, looked at the wall beyond the blocks and, after several moments of wild thought, said with great delight,

> 'I know . . . I know . . . it's 3 lots of SIX as well!'

The exciting thing for me was that Robert didn't look at the blocks at all. He looked at the wall *beyond* while he was deliberating. He seemed to be working from an internal model that was beginning to form – presumably as a result of the high level of concentration needed in order to solve the problems visually.

Once the concept of division was established, we linked the blocks with his tables book. Each time he divided a set of blocks visually, he looked up the result in the relevant table. Gradually the mysteries of the tables book were revealed and we progressed to more formal work from there!

Robert had mastered division but he had also learned a useful range of number facts as well. I feel that tasks similar to this could be devised to help dyslexic youngsters improve their sense of number. The key ingredients appear to be – a fusion of number language with its concrete counterpart combined with a high level of challenge and concentration.

More advanced concepts – with Jonathan

Jonathan and his mother sat down for a lesson. 'I know you want to do the "ough" words today', his mother said, 'but you'll have to help us with Jonathan's Maths homework. We stayed up for hours last night trying to explain $2n + 1 = 9$ but he just can't see what the "n" means!'

I set out a problem with Dienes blocks and hid two blocks in a little plastic box as part of the sum.

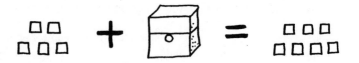

'How many blocks are there in the box?'

Jonathan smiled. There were obviously two. I set up a second problem. . . . But this time he held back, his eyes thoughtfully dwelling on the blocks and his mind on something else. Then he quickly solved my problem and from then on insisted on setting problems for *us* to solve instead. And very ingenious they were! He quickly introduced '$2n$' (these were 2 boxes) and then explored the possibilities of different amounts in each box, these were labelled 'n' and 'm'. Soon, he was confidently doing his homework without needing any extra help from us at all.

We had not actually taught Jonathan anything. From the moment I set out the first problem in blocks he took over. He explored the idea himself by inventing problems for us to solve and then quietly got on with his homework without any apparent difficulty. He seemed to have no trouble grasping the relationships once these were made more concrete.

On a similar occasion, he was unable to solve problems to do with angles in a circle.

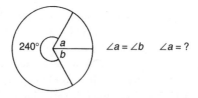

Jonathan knew there were 360 degrees in a circle but he could not see what to do with the 240. His parents had gone to great lengths trying to explain but he seemed unwilling to accept this. Perhaps, like other dyslexics, he had learnt that unless he understood what he was doing it was no good – he would eventually forget. So because he was unable to see where the 240 fitted in, he could not simply accept their explanation as another child might do.

I had planned to tackle this with lentils. It was a rather homespun analogy but it was all that I could think of at the time! I tipped some lentils into a saucer and asked Jonathan to count out 360, very roughly, and spread them in a circle. This took him quite a while. I had intended to take out a sector from the circle and develop the explanation from there, but Jonathan stopped me. He had *seen* what to do. It was obvious, and he wanted to get on with his homework straightaway.

The questions progressed quite quickly in difficulty, covering a range of problems involving general angle properties. Jonathan worked quietly on his own. Occasionally his eyes strayed to the lentils as if seeking support, but the problems were quite clear to him and he required no extra help from us.

It was as though he could not 'think' 360 degrees – this was too intangible. But he could think in terms of lentils and counting out 360 lentils was enough to make the problem sufficiently concrete for him to grasp. This was all he needed. From then on everything fell into place and he was able to continue on his own.

The Dienes blocks in '$2n + 1 = 9$' had played a similar role. In both these situations Jonathan's ability to understand mathematical relationships was good. What he could not do so well was grasp them in a purely abstract way. He needed concrete support.

As a dyslexic child gets older, he may not need to develop new concepts in concrete situations in the way that younger children do. But the weakness in verbal thinking may still be there. If he asks for help, explaining to him *in words* may only make things worse and add to his confusion. It may be better to present the problem in a concrete form and allow him to see the relationships in this way.

Making symbols meaningful

'×' is linked to 'lots of' which in turn is linked to the rows of pins . . .

I would like to end with a tale about young Gemma and her fear of symbols. Gemma had built up her $3\times$ table with map-pins (described earlier for Daniel) and was familiar with the phrase 'lots of' and the formal symbol '×'.

She was working through a computer program in which 'lots of' was gradually juxtaposed with the symbol and then finally replaced by it altogether. She would work away quite happily until the symbol '×' first appeared on the screen. Each time the symbol appeared she quietly walked away from the computer and did something else. And if we attempted to explain the symbol, she very politely changed the subject!

What to do? Gemma, her mother and I played a simple game. We sat in a circle and I asked her, 'What's 2 lots of 3?' 'Six!' Then Gemma asked her mother, 'What's 3 lots of 3?' 'Nine', and so on. Each time we said 'lots of' we crossed our arms in the shape of a multiplication sign. It took the form of a children's song-and-gesture game. We linked the words 'lots of' to the *feel* of a diagonal cross. Then we drew them with coloured pens and called them 'lots of' signs. This worked. The next time Gemma tackled the computer program she responded to the symbol without a murmur!

Gemma showed the same evasive fear for the symbol for division, but I was prepared this time. On our large hand-written worksheets we did this – at the end of each page I asked her to find all the words 'divide' and turn the two dots into big round ones by going over them with a pen. This was fun. They got bigger and bigger and then became brightly coloured. By the time we got to the sixth sheet the dots were an all-important part of the work.

The link between

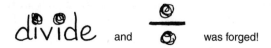

CONCLUSION

In this chapter, I have tried to show that, because of a generalized weakness in language, dyslexic children may have difficulty acquiring mathematical concepts in the normal way. It may be easier for them if they are allowed to explore new ideas with concrete materials and develop their understanding in this way.

This means that in a mathematics class a dyslexic youngster will have different needs. He may be tackling the same work as the other children, yet still require the kind of concrete support we usually associate with a much younger or less able child.

All the children I have described had had years and years of careful patient teaching. It was puzzling how quickly they forgot. We felt that yet more explanation followed by the usual written practice was unlikely to work. We would simply be repeating what had gone before.

Instead, we created opportunities for them to develop their thinking with concrete materials and we strengthened the language they would need. This seems to have helped. The *understanding* that is released by this change of approach has surprised us all.

ACKNOWLEDGEMENT

I am grateful to Chris Weeks, my former Open University tutor, for reading this chapter and providing helpful suggestions.

NOTES

1. Dienes blocks are used in most primary schools and are obtainable from the main educational suppliers.

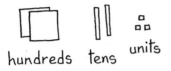

hundreds   tens   units

2. 'Embedded' – I use this term in the sense intended by Margaret Donaldson in her book *Children's Minds*, London, Fontana, 1978.

Chapter 4

Reading and writing in mathematics

Elaine Miles

To speak of dyslexic children having 'mathematical' difficulties may obscure the fact that many of these difficulties are of a linguistic nature and are therefore not unexpected in view of their particular weaknesses in the literacy field. There are a great many different points at which such weaknesses may affect their mathematics, and my chief object in this chapter is to survey them, although occasionally I may briefly suggest some way of helping.

DIFFICULTIES WITH THE TEXT OF A PROBLEM

The first thought that springs to mind, given the title of this chapter, is that dyslexic children may be handicapped in reading the text of problems. If an ordinary situation is being described, such as building a bookcase or papering the walls of a room, a certain level of reading skill is assumed; and it may be extra hard for the dyslexic if the setter attempts to make the problem interesting by choosing less everyday objects as the subjects of the problem, for example by asking the price of a number of 'embroidery skeins' instead of 'pencils' or by asking how long it will take to drive from Avignon to Chalons at a given speed rather than from Leeds to Bradford – since these pose extra decoding puzzles. The dyslexic may also be bothered by longer unfamiliar words chosen to give greater mathematical precision, such as 'dimensions' used instead of 'size'.

Perhaps less obvious a difficulty is the fact that the approach to reading required is not that to which he is accustomed, although this may not have been made clear by his teachers. He is perhaps practised in getting the gist of a story. Being used, then, to concentrate on what is happening, he is now, on the contrary, expected to ignore the narrative and look for relationships. Having read the problem through and perhaps been reminded of the bookcase at home or of the time when his father papered the hall, in the examples

I suggested earlier, he may be no nearer understanding what sort of sum is needed, because he is not focusing on the right things. In this situation, to draw a picture of the bookcase or the room may help him to pick out the essentials of what is required. Another helpful device is for him to rewrite the question in his own words.

It is common practice to tell a child, when tackling a problem, to look first to see what is 'given'. However, what is 'given' will be found in small details scattered around the text, just like those 'little words' which in his previous reading experience he has been most accustomed to overlook, for example,

45 cm, 54°

Labelling the picture which he has drawn will force him to go back and look at these details carefully.

The style of a sentence in a mathematical problem is often tortuous and condensed, and therefore difficult to construe, for example,

'The perimeter of a rectangular piece of paper is 4.8 cm.'

Brief and to the point? However, the first thing that we need to pick out is that it is a *rectangular* piece of paper; only then is the word 'perimeter' meaningful. Yet the word 'rectangular' is buried in the middle of the sentence.

There is also a major difficulty about vocabulary. In all his reading in mathematics, not only of problems, but also of the explanations which he finds in his class mathematics book, he will find a plethora of technical terms, since each new topic brings a fresh collection of them. They are of two types: there are the ones which are deceptively familiar but used in a quite different sense from the one that he associates with them, and there are the much more lengthy ones which are totally new.

Examples of the first type are the following, with the associations that the child is likely to bring to them:

makes	(mother makes a cake)
take away	(Chinese take-away)
odd	(something peculiar)
even	(the game is very even)
set	(tea-set)
square	(meet me in the square)
power	(there's been a power cut)

division   (Liverpool is in the first division)
dividend   (what Dad hopes to get from the pools)
index   (look it up at the back of the book)
compass   (take it with you on Dartmoor)
vulgar   (!)
improper   (!)

In everyday life these words either have much less exact meanings than those demanded by their mathematical use, or may even have totally different associations; either way confusion is likely. The town square that the child knows is of indefinite shape; food bought at a 'Chinese take-away' is totally removed, and taking always involves discrete objects. The concept of 'division' as a mathematical operation is far from the thoughts of a young football fan. Such vivid associations are not easily dispelled merely by rote learning of phrases, for example 'An even number is one which is divisible by two.' In this case the terms 'even number' and 'odd number' may need to be illustrated spatially for the full implications to be seen by a child who naturally thinks in spatial terms, perhaps in some such way as this (Figure 4.1).

Even the words 'write/right' may be a source of confusion, as reported by one who was herself a dyslexic (Street 1976):

> Write it down.
> You haven't got it right.
> Put the 1 right up at the top.
> Now make that right.
> Put it on the right.
> Right, now we'll do another one.

The second set of mathematical terms are those which are likely to appear quite alien to the child, and the relevance of the underlying concept to the sums involved will quite likely not be grasped at all. Such words become

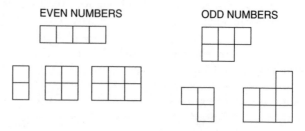

Figure 4.1 Spatial illustration of even and odd numbers

difficult for the dyslexic to remember in detail and therefore to spell; nor are they of any use to him in performing the mathematical operations. Examples are:

numerator	quadrilateral	quotient
denominator	simultaneous	vector
isosceles	proportion	coefficient
hypotenuse	binary	ratio

How, for instance, is one supposed to remember which term is which of 'numerator' and 'denominator', even with a classical education to help with the derivations? Yet one can perfectly understand, without using these terms, what the top and bottom numbers in a fraction each stand for. The word 'isosceles' is particularly puzzling. No word that the child has ever met has either of the parts of the word 'isosceles', 'iso-', or 'scel-', to help him determine how to spell it. A correspondence in *The Times* on the subject resulted in a list of 270 different ways of spelling this word taken from the work of schoolchildren. We treasure the list which was sent to us by Brian Cook who was responsible for collecting most of them. Here are a few examples which illustrate the point well. Most are phonetically acceptable.

aesosaleis	isosalise	oisossilies
aysosalease	isosyles	nicoselise
hysosiles	issossiloese	nysosalis

Two of these examples ('nicoselise' and 'nysosalis') presumably come from children who did not appreciate where words divided in 'an isosceles triangle'. An extra complication about this word is that in talking about *all three* sides being equal the term 'equilateral' is used, but when we want to say that *two* sides are equal we have to use another word from a different root; yet 'iso-' and 'equi-' in fact mean the same thing! Virtually all the words in my second list (the unfamiliar technical terms) have no word in common use from the same root to compare for spelling purposes.

I remember the word 'proportion' causing terrible trouble for one pupil whom I taught. She professed to be unable to do 'proportion' sums at all and asked to have them explained to her. In a practical situation, away from the terminology, working out how much five pencils will cost when seven cost 28p seems simple enough, and I came to the conclusion that it was the technical term which was blinding her to the obvious. Using more technical terms than necessary is putting obstacles in the way of understanding for the dyslexic. Perhaps we should consider using only those which are essential.

Finally there is the problem that the same operation may be signalled by a large variety of everyday terms. Thus 'altogether', 'total', 'sum', 'plus', 'add' and 'and' must all equally be interpreted as 'addition sum needed here', while – perhaps even more perplexing – 'minus', 'difference', and 'how much more?' must all be taken to mean 'do a subtraction sum'. They are all being used as technical terms, although they do not appear to be. The child probably needs to be specifically alerted to the range of expressions like this that will indicate to him what he has to *do* when he starts to think in terms of sums.

DIFFICULTIES WITH THE SYMBOLIC LANGUAGE OF MATHEMATICS

The arabic numerals

So far we have been talking only about difficulties associated with use of the alphabetic symbolization which the child has met in his reading books. But mathematics has its own symbolic language, which has to be learned. For the dyslexic, pushing numbers about without understanding their function will prove no more successful than pushing letters about unthinkingly when he was dealing with the alphabet, and will result in similar muddles with their order and in possible confusion between those of similar visual appearance, for example 5 and 8.

Position is even more important in mathematics than it is in spelling. Whereas the teacher may possibly guess that you mean 'brain' when you write 'brian', because the latter is not a noun of wide application and needs a capital letter to be meaningful, it is not likely that she will realize that you mean '1,438' when you write '1,348'; and when the error has been compounded by addition or subtraction there is total chaos. Although nowadays, in the early stages of mathematics, teachers are encouraged to do practical work with concrete objects to give the basis for number concepts, this may not have been enough for the dyslexic, or may have come at too early a stage for him to learn from it. He is then pushed on with the others to doing *what the teacher tells him to do* without having grasped why. This is especially true of carrying figures. Teacher tells him to put a little figure 1 at the top, so he does. Henceforward he expects any little working number at the top to be a 1.

Small differences in the position of numbers are also sometimes used to mark important distinctions in mathematics. Consider these series, which are given in a cheap book of 'Home Tests' – part of a so-called intelligence test:

22. 1. 2. 3. 4.
23. 1. 4. 7. 10.
24. 3. 4. 6. 9.
25. 35. 30. 25. 20.

The child has to continue the series. He must be careful to realize that the first number is the number of the question and therefore not to be included, especially in the fourth case, where it is tempting to do so. A clearly laid out page is particularly important for the dyslexic. Another source of bewilderment is the important differences signalled by size and position, for example,

$$23 \qquad 22.3 \qquad 22^3 \; (10648) \qquad 22_3 \; (8)$$

The symbolization of fractions is something particularly difficult to grasp, because numbers in fractions cannot be treated exactly the same way as whole numbers, but this is not always realized. Consequently the dyslexic will readily use an inappropriate algorithm, as in this example given to me once by a teacher in New Zealand (Figure 4.2).

In fact the girl has used a consistent method throughout, but it was one appropriate to cancellation of factors rather than subtraction. For having chosen a common denominator perfectly correctly (even if at times an unnecessarily high one) she then did a subtraction sum diagonally between the numerator of one fraction and the denominator of the other, in either direction, rather as one does when dividing by common factors. The working, on that principle, is perfectly correct.

$$\frac{5}{6} - \frac{1}{3} = \frac{2}{12} - \frac{5}{12} = \frac{3}{12}$$

$$\frac{7}{8} - \frac{3}{4} = \frac{3}{16} - \frac{5}{16} = \frac{3}{16}$$

$$\frac{8}{9} - \frac{1}{2} = \frac{6}{18} - \frac{8}{18} = \frac{2}{18}$$

Figure 4.2 A multiplication procedure has been used for a subtraction sum

Particular difficulties will also arise from the dyslexic's confusion over direction and his general inflexibility of approach. In following a text in a reading book, the pupil has been taught to move from left to right. In mathematics he must be flexible, depending on the operation required. If he understands base 10 properly because of having had experience with concrete materials, he will appreciate that in doing addition and multiplication sums he must do the right-hand column first because he may have to 'trade' if he has more than 10, and these 'tens' need to be included in the next column to the left when he gets to it. That is the reason why it is usual to work from the right. A dyslexic child has to understand explicitly in a way that may not be necessary for the more linguistically able members of the class, who simply accept that they have to work in a particular direction.

In dealing with an equation, on the other hand, the mathematical equivalent of a sentence, he must be prepared to read it from left to right *or* right to left according to what he needs to do. If, for instance, this pupil has always read:

$$6 + 4 = \text{what?}$$

and never:

$$\text{what} - 4 = 6?$$

or:

$$10 - \text{what} = 6?$$

which would train him to see how these operations are interchangeable, he will not be able to 'juggle about' with figures – for example, using the commutative principle to make multiplication sums easier; thus:

$$3 \times 7 \text{ is the same as } 7 \times 3$$

He may be unsure about the $7\times$ table but completely confident about the $3\times$ table. This is very important for the dyslexic, for whom multiplication tables are a major source of difficulty.

Algebraic symbols

Such flexibility with regard to direction is very important for algebra. The dyslexic may be completely at a loss what to do when he sees:

$$x - 5 = 16$$

unless of course he can recognize it as the same type of sentence as the one he met earlier:

$$\text{what} - 5 = 16?$$

Both are in effect asking 'What number can you take 5 from and leave 16?' Dyslexics are not alone in having difficulty in coping with equations, but they are particularly vulnerable to this sort of difficulty where the task demands flexibility and a sense of direction.

There are also other problems with algebraic notation. Algebraic equations are often a shorthand way of saying two things at once and these have to be separated out and dealt with in turn; thus:

$$3x - 5 = 16$$

is saying *both* that there is a number ($3x$) which is 5 more than 16 *and* that the number that we are really seeking is a third of that number. The pupil has to understand that $3x$ is itself a number, which has to be worked out first.

The notation for such numbers is also different from the arithmetical one. Thirty-five means three tens and five units, but $3x$ means three times x; with algebraic symbols multiplication signs are not used – the number and the algebraic symbol are just put next to each other. Similarly $(a + b)(a + b)$ means $(a + b)$ times $(a + b)$, with the bracket holding the complex number together. Such a complex expression is very difficult to understand, but a spatially inclined pupil may understand it perfectly if shown a diagram like the following (Figure 4.3) which illustrates $(a + b)(a + b)$ as representing an area of an enlarged square, originally with a side of length 'a', to which has been added an extension in each direction of length 'b' to form a square of side '$a + b$'. It is easy then to see how the new total area is expressed by $a^2 + 2ab + b^2$, the sum of the area of four different pieces.

Dienes (1960) uses just such a method to demonstrate the meaning of algebraic concepts.

Even at a more sophisticated level there is always the difficulty of understanding how a symbol for a variable differs from a symbol acting as a name.

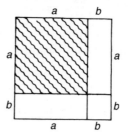

Figure 4.3 Spatial illustration of $(a + b)(a + b)$

A striking example of this is given by Mestre and Gerace (1986) in a question which they set to 14-year-old maths students, of whom only one out of fourteen got it right.

> Mr Smith noted the number of cars, C, and the number of trucks, T, in a parking lot and wrote the following equation to represent the situation:
>
> $$8C = T$$
>
> Are there more cars or trucks in this parking lot? Why?

One would expect this problem to bother others besides dyslexics, but it is an illustration of symbols being used in different ways, alphabetically and mathematically. 'C' and 'T' do not stand for 'cars' and 'trucks', but for the *numbers* of cars and trucks respectively. The *number* of trucks is the same as eight times the *number* of cars.

Mathematical symbols other than numerals

Here the first ones which spring to mind are the ones which the child meets first, namely $+$, $-$, $\times$, $\div$, and $=$. Many mistakes are made if the first four are not clearly differentiated. It is probably valuable to explain the relationship between addition and multiplication and the relationship between subtraction and division; these are represented by the fact that the two symbols in each pair look more like each other, in each case the second one being a development from its partner. Understanding of these relationships and of the contrasting opposition of the two pairs to each other makes it more easy to remember which is which.

Difficulty over direction often gets dyslexics into trouble over the signs for 'greater than' and 'less than', namely > and <. Although others may just *remember* to draw the sign from left to right for 'more than' and the other way for 'less than', the dyslexic needs to be taught to recognize both as static figures between two numbers, with the wide 'mouth' facing the larger number, and the tiny point next to the small number, for example,

5 < 8

6 > 4

Put that way, direction does not come into it.

These are only two of the large number of extra symbols, in addition to the arabic numerals, which the budding mathematician has to learn, involving a far greater burden of paired associate learning than in learning the use of the alphabet. Mathematics also constantly makes other nice distinctions represented by tiny differences in the symbol used, for example different sorts of brackets, round, curly and straight, used in different areas of mathematics:

There are also the hoop-like symbols used in set theory to denote membership of classes. I find it particularly to the point that in a popular series of books on mathematics foundation skills for 11- to 14-year olds there is a cartoon in which a boy is gazing at some shelf brackets and the teacher is saying 'not *that* sort of brackets!'

If we take into account how in these many different ways linguistic facility is needed in the building of basic arithmetical skills, we shall apply some of the same techniques in helping dyslexics with their mathematics that we do in teaching them literacy skills; that is we have to make quite clear what function the symbols are performing, without taking anything for granted.

It is, of course, quite true that children other than dyslexics may suffer from some of the difficulties which I have mentioned. What is important is that we separate out the linguistic components of mathematical difficulties and deal with them explicitly when that is needed. As we know, dyslexics are particularly vulnerable in linguistic areas.

Let me end with an example given by a dyslexic (Street 1976) of the confusion caused mainly by what the teacher is *saying* to her. The author uses capitals to indicate the words over which she had to stop and think.

We are going to TAKE 25 FROM 61. WRITE DOWN 61 first (I sometimes wrote the first figure I heard before the second one.) WRITE DOWN 25 UNDERNEATH it. Put the 2 UNDER the 6 and the 5 UNDER the 1. Draw a line UNDERNEATH. Start at the bottom on the RIGHT. Take 5 AWAY FROM 1. It won't go. Start again. Borrow 10 FROM the 6. (Confusion here because you take smaller numbers from bigger ones, and 10 take away 6 is 4.) 'Where do I put the 4?' There isn't a 4 in the sum. Now pay attention . . . start again. You are borrowing 10 FROM 60. (Confusion again because that seems to leave a 50 somewhere.) You borrow the 10 from the 60 and add it to the 1 to make 11. Then you take the 5 AWAY FROM 11. That leaves 6. Put the 6 DOWN, UNDER the line BELOW the 5. There is no need to take so long. Take the one you have borrowed AWAY FROM the 6. 'Which 6?'. Then take 2 AWAY FROM the 6. 'Which 6?'. Then take 2 AWAY FROM 5. That leaves 3. If you like you can pay back the 10 to the 2 and that makes 3. Then you take 3 AWAY FROM 6, and you get the same answer, 3. Put the 3 DOWN, on the LEFT of the 6. Not that 6, the one in your answer. Read the answer from LEFT to RIGHT – 36.

Eventually Street taught herself to subtract by her own private method (which involved adding), despite the disapproval of her teacher who said that this method was too confusing!

REFERENCES

Dienes, Z.P. (1960) *Building up Mathematics*, London, Hutchinson Educational.
Mestre, J. and Gerace, W. (1986) 'The interplay of linguistic factors in mathematical translation tasks', *Focus on Learning Problems in Mathematics*, 8(1), 59–72.
Street, J. (1976) 'Sequencing and directional confusion in arithmetic', *Dyslexia Review*, 15, 16–19.

Chapter 5

Difficulties at the secondary stage

Anne Henderson

INTRODUCTION

According to Steeves (1983) and Joffe (1981) many dyslexics have much potential to succeed in mathematics once they have grasped the basic concepts. In fact some dyslexics are capable of scaling great heights with their mathematical prowess. With this in mind a teacher should never underestimate potential and should try to ensure that opportunities for advanced goals are available should students want them. Once a concept is mastered fully, to ask a pupil to complete pages and pages of similar problems is a waste of time. He should be given the chance to move on.

DEALING WITH THE TENSION

Fear and anxiety associated with mathematics are often magnified in a dyslexic pupil. In the case of my own work, which was mostly with dyslexics aged between 11 and 16, at first I regularly saw them in a one-to-one teaching situation; and if they did not know me they might well conclude that their 'stupidity' (as they see it) would be exposed. Even though many of them would have been told that they are *not* just 'stupid' they might still be lacking in confidence and be unable to shake off the belief that they are going to fail. I once had a pupil who came to me, white-faced and stiff-backed, who proceeded to grip the pencil with hot sweaty hands, and who showed not just fear but sheer panic. A first lesson in this atmosphere is a tough experience for pupil and teacher alike.

To be effective in this kind of situation a teacher needs to have confidence in her own abilities to help. This in turn enhances the pupil's confidence. Encouraging the pupil to talk about himself and to discuss the way he sees his maths problem is a good way of beginning a working relationship. Allowing the pupil to mention past failures and incidents that have embarrassed him with regard to his dyslexia is a way of improving this relationship.

It also helps if the pupil and teacher can discuss a topic common to both of them, possibly a school trip, a school activity, or even some outside event with which they are both familiar. A game in the lesson may help to ease the atmosphere, since the emphasis is not so much on the pupil as on playing the game, and this is a way of taking the pressure out of a one-to-one situation. Using a game to start a lesson heightens a pupil's awareness of number and also helps to prevent any anxiety he may feel about his lack of ability at the subject. Allowing a pupil to discuss and talk freely about his problems gives him the opportunity to express and to show his own strengths and weaknesses. Humour, too, is something that eases anxious moments and enables the pupil to relax.

It is necessary to identify the place where the pupil is in his mathematics education and to start helping him at that point. The teacher should observe the pupil to see his reactions to certain mathematical topics. Having long-term goals with short-term objectives can be helpful. Dyslexic children are difficult to assess, since the pace at which they move through a topic may vary, and some have an extraordinary potential to 'see' answers or develop strategies for coping.

Pupils who have a specific difficulty are also individuals with their own learning style (compare this book, Chapter 2). It is interesting to observe the methods which they use and, where appropriate, to incorporate improvements. If pictorial or verbal mnemonics, or material on tape, help a student to learn a particular mathematical point, then the teacher should try to make sure that these are available as much as possible. Once a pupil finds a method by which he learns, his self-esteem is enhanced and he will have the confidence to make good progress.

When dealing with a dyslexic pupil the teacher should be fully conversant with the effect that his language difficulties are having on his mathematics. In the knowledge that sequencing and direction problems and problems of short-term memory will all be contributing to the pupil's learning difficulties, a teacher should be continually on the look-out for problematic areas and be ready to help with ideas and suggestions. Identification of a problem is not easy, but if a teacher is aware of its existence she can be on the alert. Emphasizing strengths is not new to teaching; but when a pupil has failed many times it is vitally important to build up confidence by telling him – and showing him – that he is able to do something well. Even winning a little game and beating the teacher is enough to start a growth of self-esteem. Encouraging his success and calling attention to work that has been well done will contribute further to promoting his confidence.

EXAMPLES OF DIFFICULTIES

Sometimes the pupil will discuss correctly the method that he has used. Then several problems are worked through orally, and he will go through each stage step by step, showing clearly that he understands the concept. Even when a slightly different calculation arises he will deal with it quite competently and tell the teacher exactly what needs to be done. Yet, when it comes to doing the calculation, even with the aid of a calculator, he comes up with the wrong answer. The teacher discusses the method once more; the computation is repeated – and the answer is wrong again! The teacher will eventually discover that, although the pupil is *saying* the correct word, for example, 'multiply', he will be pressing the 'divide' button on the calculator. This sends the whole calculation wrong. The following is an example of precisely this mistake:

One of my pupils, Bob, aged 14, was given the following question:

> A factory worker earns a basic pay of £3.20 an hour for a 36-hour week. For any extra hours he is paid time and a half. Calculate his earnings if he works for 39 hours.

This is what he said he would do:

> £3.20 for 36 hours = £3.20 × 36 = £115.20
> To find time and a half divide the £3.20 by 2 = £1.60
> Add this £1.60 to the £3.20 = £4.80
> Multiply £4.80 by 3 = £14.40
> Total £115.20 + £14.40 = £129.60

But this is what he did:

> £3.20 × 36 = £115.20
> £3.20 ÷ 2 = £1.60
> £1.60 + £3.20 = £4.80

So far so good. But the next step was £4.80 × 3. Here he pressed the ÷ button, and he was so engrossed that he was not aware of this error! Since £4.80 ÷ 3 came to £1.60 he proceeded as follows:

> £1.60 + £115.20 = £116.80

The answer was wrong, but his understanding of the concepts was entirely correct.

Here is a similar example but at a more advanced level. Mark, aged 15, had been given the following problem in trigonometry:

A triangle, CBN, has angle N the right-angle; angle B is 28°, and the hypotenuse, BC, is 3 metres. What is the length of CN and BN?

Mark drew the triangle correctly; he then thought out the formulae for *sine* and *cosine*, namely that 'sine' is 'opposite over hypotenuse' and 'cosine' is 'adjacent over hypotenuse'. This gave him:

$$\sin 28° = \frac{CN}{3}$$

This gave him that CN was 1.4 metres.

He then repeated the procedure, and wrote:

$$\cos 28° = \frac{BN}{3}$$

When he came to do the calculation, however, *he copied the value of sin 28° over again*! This meant that BN was also 1.4 metres, which was clearly absurd. On these and similar occasions it is worth reminding the pupil that he should not simply equate 'wrong answer' with failure or see the situation simply as another setback. He has in fact gone most of the way towards solving the problem and has understood the important points.

Another difficulty for dyslexics is the recognition of the decimal point within a number. One thing that can go wrong is that the comma dividing off the thousands is often mistaken for the real decimal point. Using a big red plastic decimal point can emphasize its place and also give the pupil a tactile object to reinforce his knowledge. With amounts involving money a pupil may recognize the amount orally, but may have difficulty in punching the correct amount into the calculator. Problems arise with values of pounds and single unit pence, for example, £1.06 or £6.07, which the pupil may punch in as '£1.60' or '£6.70'. Also the reverse may happen, so that a reading of £1.6 is read as 'one pound six pence', while £6.7 might be read as 'six pounds seven pence'. Sometimes a pupil will just ignore the decimal point! This can cause considerable trouble especially if the amount involved is only pence, for example, 68p. If the answer needs to be given in pence there is no problem, but if it has to be given in pounds and the student is unaware of his error then he can get into all kinds of difficulties. Here is an example which arose in the case of one of my pupils, David, aged 15.

The problem which he was asked to solve was as follows:

> A man travelled 12,000 miles in a car, buying petrol at a price of 44p per litre. If his car travelled an average of 11 miles per litre, calculate the estimated cost of the petrol used in the car, giving the correct answer to the nearest whole pound.

David recognized that if he divided 12,000 by 11 it would give the number of litres used, and he also saw that if he multiplied this number by 44p he would get the answer that he needed. He highlighted the symbols so as to clarify the procedures:

$\div$ $12,000 \div 11 = 1090.9091$

$\times$ $1090.9091 \times 44p$

He punched in 44 but forgot that the answer was in pence: the man, it seemed, spent £48,000 on petrol each year! At this point David started to panic, realizing that this answer was obviously wrong. Like many others in a stress situation he then came up with a wholly inappropriate suggestion, namely 'Shall I multiply 11 by 44? Will that give me a better answer?'

In such circumstances it is very easy for the teacher to show impatience or at least disappointment. What is needed may in fact be an encouraging smile or a 'Don't worry', since these will help him to relax. Teacher and pupil can then work together in discovering where the pupil went wrong and working out strategies which will enable him to avoid similar mistakes in the future. Where a single error leads to an absurd result it is important to remind him that there is nothing wrong with his understanding of what is needed and that if he continues to make occasional errors of this kind this is a tiresome complication but is in no way evidence that he is 'no good at maths'.

Because of the dyslexic's distinctive weaknesses, the symbol/language connection needs to be talked about continually. Wall charts can be provided, as well as cards which the pupil can carry around with him and use for reference. Any mathematical terms which the pupil will encounter within a particular topic should be discussed and written down before the topic is begun. This can help avoid the anxious moments which can arise if the word is encountered and not understood. Teachers can build up vocabulary lists for the individual pupil, and these can be related not only to important words in mathematics but to other curriculum subjects. A pupil can print out his list on a word processor and can share his work with others. Creating a folder to which all pupils can contribute is often a good idea: it makes an interesting project, and, since it is cross-curricular, enthusiasm may spread to other subjects.

In dealing with fractions, for example, it is useful gradually to introduce the pupil to words connected with the topic, for example 'parts', 'groups', 'divide', 'vulgar', 'improper', 'denominator', 'numerator', and so on. This will be a safeguard against later panic.

There are some dyslexics who are very good at mental arithmetic and are able to work out the answer in double-quick time. However, in the GCSE examination points are given for method. This means that, even though their answer is correct, if they do not record their working they will lose marks. For many pupils writing down a process in little stages is the easy part of a computation; for a dyslexic it is likely to be the part which he finds most difficult. He may give the correct answer – then, when he picks up a pen and begins to write, he crosses out, starts again, swallows hard, gets sweaty hands, makes yet another mistake – and decides that the whole thing is too much for him. In cases such as this it could even be a good idea to tell the pupil to go through the whole paper putting down answers and then come back and begin to record those methods which he is able to explain.

Sometimes in mathematics, if the calculation involves big numbers, fractions or decimal points, the student is shown how to round off the numbers so as to make the computation simpler. Teaching him to use 'easy' numbers – for example numbers without decimal points – can help him to grasp a particular concept more fully. Thus:

$$526.3 \div 47.61$$

might be written as:

$$500 \div 50$$

Hence the answer to the sum is approximately 10. Many dyslexic pupils will see the point of doing the rounding off, discuss the method in detail and agree wholeheartedly with it. But when a problem arises that is slightly different a pupil may be influenced by the differences in wording or presentation of the problem and fail to use the approximated answer properly.

The following was a problem which I gave to William, one of my pupils aged 14:

15 pencils are in a pack that is 20 cm wide.
How thick is each pencil?

I suggested, in the usual way, that it might help him if he thought in terms of simpler numbers in the first place, and I therefore said to him: '3 pencils are in a pack that is 6 cm wide. How thick is each pencil?' He saw that the answer was 2 cm and returned to the original problem. There was a long pause. In my naïvety I was totally bewildered by this. I had, as I thought, shown him quite clearly what to do and could not understand his hesitation. Finally he said to me, 'How can these pencils change width? If they were 2 cm there' (referring to my 'simpler' example), 'how can they be different now?' I realized that instead of clarifying the situation I had actually made it more complicated.

I had a similar experience with Richard, who was aged 16. We were dealing with pie charts when the following problem arose:

If 360 degrees represent £1,000 what does 1 degree represent?

Richard proceeded to do the following computation:

$$360 \div 1,000 = 0.36$$

He realized, however, that this was wrong, having estimated that each degree of the 'pie' must have a value of about £3. I therefore tried to help him by using simpler numbers: 'if $10°$ represents £20 what does $1°$ represent?' He immediately gave the correct answer, £2, and realized that he had divided the £20 by the number of degrees. He then solved the earlier problem without any trouble. After this, however, we passed on to another problem in which $40°$ represented 600 cars. Richard then asked, 'How can 1 degree represent 15 cars when' (pointing to $1° = £2$) 'we proved that 1 degree was £2?'

This apparent inability to adjust to new situations can cause confusion in many different topics.

A similar point is illustrated in the case of Matthew, who was aged 14. He had been working out the areas of triangles through practical work – by drawing them and by cutting them up to make rectangles; and we had agreed that to find the area of a triangle was in fact very easy since all that was needed was:

$\frac{1}{2}$ the base $\times$ the height

Matthew seemed very confident and used the formula many times successfully. I thought that he had mastered and understood the concept. However, much later, when we were doing some revision on this same topic, he got into difficulty. Trying to jog his memory I mentioned the practical work that we had done previously and talked about cutting up triangles to find their areas. Matthew said quite emphatically that using the formula 'half base times height' was applicable only when equilateral triangles were involved – that was the only example which he had remembered from the previous work; all the other examples which he had completed successfully had been forgotten.

Transferring a method from one calculation to another seems too much for them. Once a method has seemingly been grasped, a pupil will energetically set down the next problem, taking great care to do things properly; then he will exactly copy a part of the previous one which has got absolutely nothing to do with the present one.

Throughout this work the basic difficulties seem to be connected to the four 'operators', '+', '−', '×' and '÷'. At least one and more often two or more are required to complete a computation, and it is essential that the pupil should be able to identify and understand the processes that each one signifies. Although it is plain from the examples given here that these four symbols are very important, equally important is the '=' symbol; this is used just as frequently as the others but is rarely talked about.

THE '=' SIGN

Children meet the 'equals' sign early in their education and the language associated with it starts at this stage. They may come across the word 'is', 'the same as', 'means', 'is equivalent to', and so on. Perhaps their first encounter with it is in a simple equation in the infant department:

$$1 + 2 = 3 \quad \text{or} \quad 6 - 4 = 2$$

As a pupil progresses through school he may meet the symbol every day in connection, not only with mathematics, but also with other subjects across the curriculum. Eventually he will meet it formally in algebra. At this point the dyslexic child may well feel sure that he will never be able to understand it because by this time letters are causing problems and when they appear in a problem alongside numbers the difficulty is compounded. From observations of older pupils, especially those reaching GCSE levels, it has become apparent that 'understanding' the meaning of an equation is something which they have never managed. Although they have written the symbol '=' every day for many years its actual mathematical meaning has eluded them. In finding methods of helping individual pupils who are trying to cope with Pythagoras's theorem or trigonometrical ratios but have never been able to manipulate values on different sides of equations, a return to basics is essential. The area is one in which the typical difficulties of the dyslexic clearly show themselves.

It is important to check in the first place that the pupil is familiar with some of the basic principles of algebra. These are:

  (i) 'x' is the same as '$+1x$',
 (ii) '$2x$' means '2 multiply by x',
(iii) a bracket means 'multiply',
 (iv) the commutative principle applies to both '$+$' and '$\times$'. Thus '1×2' is the same as '2×1' and '$1 + 2$' is the same as '$2 + 1$' (but '$1 \div 2$' is not the same as '$2 \div 1$' and '$1 - 2$' is not the same as '$2 - 1$').

There are two different ways of explaining how the '$=$' sign works in the solving of equations. In the first place it can be thought of as a balance which must be kept level at all times. In that case, if something is done to one side of the equation, then precisely the same thing must be done to the other. Second, the pupil can be shown how it is that the mathematical symbols all have opposite values when they are moved through the '$=$' sign on to the opposite side of the equation. Here is an example:

> Find the value of x in the following equation:
> $3x - 2 = x + 12$

If the first method is used a record can be kept of all the things that are done to both sides. The working might then look like this:

$$
\begin{aligned}
3x - 2 &= x + 12 \\
3x - 2 + 2 &= x + 12 + 2 \qquad (+2) \\
3x &= x + 14 \\
3x - x &= x + 14 - x \qquad (-x) \\
2x &= 14 \\
x &= 7 \qquad (\div 2)
\end{aligned}
$$

If the second method is used the following principles apply:

$+$	becomes	$-$
$-$	becomes	$+$
$\times$	becomes	$\div$
$\div$	becomes	$\times$

We start, as before, with the original equation:

$$3x - 2 = x + 12$$

Then we start to move an item to the other side:

-2 becomes $+2$, therefore	$3x = x + 12 + 2$
therefore	$3x = x + 14$
$+x$ becomes $-x$, therefore	$3x - x = 14$
therefore	$2x = 14$
$\times 2$ becomes $\div 2$, therefore	$x = 14 \div 2$
therefore	$x = 7$

Once the pupil has decided on a method to tackle a problem (whether the first or the second of these methods) he should be allowed to proceed at his own pace without interference.

Various difficulties, however, may show themselves. Thus:

(i) If a pupil has solved an equation successfully by means of the second method (for instance by moving -2 across the equation so that it becomes $+2$), then when he starts to do the next equation he will look back to see how he began the previous one and may copy not only the method but also the actual digits involved.

(ii) He may forget that $2x$ is '2 times x' and simply take away the 2 to leave x.

(iii) He may forget which symbol is the opposite of the one which he is considering, for instance, by thinking of $-$ as $\div$; or he may be concentrating so hard on remembering which is the 'opposite' that he may forget to move the value to the other side.

(iv) When using the first method he may add 2 to one side and forget to add it to the other.

(v) Sometimes he may connect the symbols '$+$' and '$-$' to the preceding letter. Thus $3x - x$ would be read as $-3x + x$.

If the teacher is aware of the possible errors and emphasizes the appropriate details it is possible to pre-empt some of these difficulties, even if not all of them. Once a pupil has a good grasp of equations it gives him confidence in other subjects across the curriculum where they occur, such as physics, chemistry and biology. It also means that mathematical formulae, for example, $C = 2\pi r$ or $A = \pi r$, or trigonometrical ratios or time/speed ratios, do not create such anxiety as before, because the pupil has acquired several strategies to help him 'find a way' through to solving a problem. Knowing he is able to attack a problem in different ways gives him a flexibility of approach which does not restrict him and which therefore gives him confidence.

One pupil said: 'Now I know a lot of little ways through I try out different ones till I can find the right answer.' Another pupil said; 'Because I know there is not just one way of finding an answer, which I usually can't remember, I search for another method I understand, instead of giving up.'

Working with a student who is keen to achieve makes the teacher aware, not only that the lesson must be interesting, but that it must contain material which will stretch the pupil's abilities and make him reach a higher level of achievement. If one is working with pupils with learning difficulties it is very easy to lower one's aims and objectives; and if a pupil thinks that his teacher does not expect him to achieve very much, then there is a tendency for the pupil not to achieve – the low aspirations of the teacher somehow permeate to the pupil.

USE OF CALCULATORS

In most examinations pupils are allowed the use of calculators. However, as has been shown already, they are liable to press the wrong symbol button because the language associated with it has confused them. A most important skill in this connection is estimation. It is necessary not only for checking computational work but in everyday life where exact answers are not necessary or are difficult to obtain.

There are various ways in which estimation can be carried out. Once a pupil begins to understand the concept then different processes can be discussed.

To round off to the nearest 10 or 100 helps the grasp of place value and enables the student to get an answer quickly. Thus:

$$48 + 43 \text{ becomes } 50 + 40 = 90$$

Reading a number on a calculator needs practice. A pupil needs to be shown how to read and correct a number to either significant figures or decimal places. As was mentioned earlier, vocabulary needs to be discussed and written down, and this applies to abbreviations also. Thus 'decimal place' might be written as 'd.pl.', 'significant figures' as 'sig.fig.' or 'S.F.'

Here are some problems that I have encountered:

(i) *Correct £706.008 to the nearest penny.*

The expected answer was £706.01, but Charles, aged 16, said that it was £706.09. His argument was that the 8 (in the .008) changed the 0 in the previous column to 9. 'The two noughts are really ten, so when I correct I make the ten go down one so that it becomes nine.' This is in effect a double error, since even if it had been correct to think of '00' as '10' he ought to have moved to 11, making the number one bigger, rather than to 9 which made it one smaller.

(ii) *Correct £32.896 to the nearest penny.*

The expected answer was £32.90, but the answer given by Tom, aged 16, was £32.18. He said that the six in the third decimal place made the nine go up one so that it became ten; thus $10 + 8 = 18$.

Much practice is necessary in correcting numbers and considering place value. If a pupil is able to estimate what is approximately the right answer, then if he presses a wrong button on the calculator he will quickly see that his answer is wrong and will retrace his steps, checking each one. In the case of complicated questions the student should be encouraged to record his estimating work and then set down his accurate work alongside so that the two can be checked. Once he gets into the habit of estimating he will do so quickly, before using his calculator; and by this means major error will probably be avoided.

CONCLUDING REMARKS

Emphasis has been placed in this chapter on the relationship between teacher and pupil. This needs to be a partnership in which both are actively involved. It is understood in particular that they will talk about the pupil's difficulties and try to discover their source. This cannot be done unless both of them are fully aware of the kinds of ways in which dyslexics are liable to go wrong. To tell a pupil that he could be successful if only he were more confident, while at the same time failing to show understanding of why he finds certain tasks difficult, is likely to diminish confidence rather than bolstering it. In contrast, if teacher and pupil work together on specific skills – the understanding of equations, estimation, the use of a calculator, and the like – this will be an encouragement to the pupil to devise other compensatory strategies as they are needed. There will be less need to panic; and he may well find that he is improving not only in mathematics but in other subjects also.

REFERENCES

Joffe, L.S. (1981) 'School mathematics and dyslexia: aspects of the interrelationship', PhD thesis, University of Aston in Birmingham.

Steeves, K.J. (1983) 'Memory as a factor in the computational efficiency of dyslexic children with high abstract reasoning ability', *Annals of Dyslexia*, 33, 141–52.

Chapter 6

The use of structured materials with older pupils

T.R. Miles

STRUCTURED MATERIALS AND SYMBOLIZATION

Dienes (1960: 31) has described mathematics as 'a structure of relationships, the formal symbolism being merely a way of communicating parts of the structure from one person to another'. Shortly afterwards (1960: 31) he speaks of 'structural relationships between concepts connected with numbers'. He then says (1960: 31–2): 'The learning of mathematics I shall take to mean the apprehension of such relationships together with their symbolisation.'

This distinction between 'apprehension of relationships' and 'symbolisation' seems to me to be of crucial importance as far as dyslexics are concerned, since they are likely to have little difficulty with the first but may well have major difficulty with the second. If they have been taught merely to memorize rules for operating with symbols then they are likely to find such memorization extremely difficult; and, as a further consequence, any sense of enjoyment or excitement at the elegance and beauty of mathematics will almost certainly be missing. Again to quote Dienes (1960: 27): 'Mathematical insights are very seldom generated on blackboards.'

We owe to Dienes in particular (and also to Montessori, Cuisenaire and Stern) the recognition that these mathematical insights are most likely to arise if the pupil is encouraged to use structured materials – rods, blocks, and so on. As is well known, Dienes himself devised what he called 'Multibase Arithmetic Blocks' (Dienes 1960: 55). The purpose of this chapter is to suggest ways in which these and similar materials can be used to help older dyslexics. Since their central problem is likely to be that of relating symbols to the operations which they represent, it is good sense that they should be able to carry out the operations first, using structured materials, and only second be shown how to describe symbolically what they have been doing.

In what follows I shall describe my work with these materials in the standard technology of 'units', 'longs', 'flats', and 'blocks'. The 'units' which

I have used have been cubes of side 1 cm; each 'long' occupies the same space as 10 'units' placed side by side; each 'flat' occupies the same space as 10 'longs' placed side by side; and a 'block' occupies the same space as 10 'flats' placed on top of each other. To indicate that the words 'units', 'longs', 'flats', and 'blocks' are being used in this specific sense I will place them in inverted commas (see also Chapter 3, note 1).

INTRODUCTION TO THE NUMBER SYSTEM

When older dyslexics, aged, say, 14 and upwards, come to me for help with their mathematics, I have sometimes found that there are some very basic points on which they have 'missed out'. Before I attempt any formal teaching I give them the chance to talk about their difficulties (just as one does in the case of literacy difficulties); and I make clear that problems with number are very common in dyslexia and that they are in fact part of the same basic limitation which has made reading and spelling difficult. It is possible, therefore, for dyslexics to use their reasoning ability, which is often high, to compensate for those weaknesses which have so far made mathematics difficult for them. I further add that, once they have mastered the basics, they may well find the subject an exciting challenge.

The purpose of introducing structured materials is not – as it is with very young children – to give them the chance to play and hence create the conditions where they make new discoveries. It is rather to set the stage for an adult-level discussion about the number system and about symbols and symbolization. In the course of the discussion it may sometimes emerge that they are still lacking in certain basic skills, for instance the ability to tell if one number is 'larger' than another or whether subtracting from a number makes that number larger or smaller. I have found it helpful not just to explain these different points as they emerge but rather to build up the pupil's understanding step by step even when some of the steps are already familiar. Just as in teaching literacy to a dyslexic one does not simply correct spelling mistakes as they occur but calls attention in a systematic way to the different ways in which speech sounds can be represented by letters of the alphabet, so in the case of mathematics, as I explain to the pupil, it is normally advisable to start at a very basic level in order to make sure that they fully understand how the number system works and how the different operations are symbolized. Once they know the meaning of familiar symbols it need not be all that daunting a task to learn the meaning of unfamiliar ones.

It is important to make clear that the tuition is being given not because they are 'failures' or 'thickies' but simply because, through no fault of their own, their dyslexia has made certain aspects of mathematics more difficult.

If this is made clear, and if it is made clear by word and gesture that one respects the pupil's intelligence, then a return to the basics of addition, and so on, need not seem childish. In just the same way many of those who teach literacy skills to older dyslexics make clear that intellectually the pupil is not at the level of 'the cat sat on the mat' but that it is useful to discuss such words if one is making a scientific study of the English spelling system. The structured materials need not be in bright colours as if they were toys; they can quite properly be regarded as scientific apparatus and should be presented as such. I have in fact often found it to be the case that someone who has spent many years of his life experiencing *lack* of success is greatly relieved when he finds himself able to produce a series of correct answers even to sums that are very simple; and once he has learned the correct algorithm he will come to be aware that he is in a position to work out the answers to any similar sum – an awareness that will do much to boost his confidence.

It is usually helpful at the start to demonstrate, step by step, what are the skills needed for understanding how the number system works. In my own case I often start by placing on the table, say, three 'units' (or any other number between one and nine) and ask the pupil to tell me 'how many' and to write down the answer in the form of an arabic numeral, namely, '3'. (In the discussions which follow I shall, for the sake of precision, use the word 'numeral' to refer to all such figures. This should not be taken to imply that the distinction between a 'numeral' and a 'number' is necessary at this stage for the pupil.) If one carries out an analysis of what this task involves it will be found to contain two elements: (i) the ability to say the correct number word ('three'), and (ii) the ability to write the correct numeral ('3').

I then add further 'units' and point out that it is possible to carry out various operations with them – adding some of them together, taking one lot away from another, putting them in a group and repeating this operation several times, and dividing a larger collection into smaller ones. The important thing for a dyslexic is to demonstrate that part of mathematics involves *doing* and that there are many different things which can be done. These include adding three 'units' to five 'units' to make eight 'units', adding four 'units' to four 'units' to make eight 'units', dividing eight 'units' into groups of four so that each group comprises two 'units', and so on. This may also be a good opportunity to explain that multiplication is repeated addition and that division is repeated subtraction.

This can then lead to the issue of notation. What I try to emphasize is that the words and symbols that we use provide an economical way of referring to these and many other operations; they therefore relate to what has been or needs to be *done*. Thus if the pupil picks out three 'units' and adds four others he will find by counting that he has seven 'units'. The total operation can be symbolized as:

$$3 + 4 = 7$$

If there is any doubt in the pupil's mind about how to carry out the four basic operations, or how to write them down, the structured materials can be used to provide practice. Stage one is to carry out the operation (add, divide, and so on) by handling the materials; stage two is to write down what has been done. It is also important to be sure that he understands the '=' sign (compare Chapter 5 of this book).

I have found that the distinction between carrying out operations and symbolizing them is often reassuring. There are, of course, plenty of operations in mathematics – for instance, calculations involving fractions, decimals, square roots, and so on – which are far more complex than adding or taking away. The important point, as one should explain, is that for dyslexics the learning of new symbols takes extra time. If in the past they have failed to understand what a particular notation was telling them to do, this can now be recognized as yet another consequence of their dyslexia; it does not follow that they are 'stupid' but only that they need to go more slowly step by step. I regularly point out to them that the principle of 'doing first – notation afterwards' is of help to dyslexics in many different contexts, since there is no problem with their ability to 'do', only with their ability to acquire and reproduce symbols at speed. In this connection music provides an interesting case for comparison, since it is possible to play or listen to a splendid time – or even to compose one – but without a suitable notation it would be impossible to communicate to others what the tune is or how it should be played. A musical score, like the symbolism of mathematics, is thus a complex form of notation for telling people what to do. Similarly written language is a notation for recording the speech sounds by means of which we communicate with each other.

With more sophisticated pupils it may be of interest to invite them to consider how one might construct alternative counting systems. For example, it would be possible, in principle, to have a system which simply consisted of the use of marks or 'tallies'. Thus instead of the symbol '5' we might write

/////

The main difficulty with such a system, however, is that we would soon run into problems if we had to deal in very large numbers. If, for instance, we needed to refer to the number 'one thousand' this would involve writing a tally mark a thousand times! This would not only be very time-consuming;

it is likely also that somewhere along the line we would 'slip one' or lose count.

There is something of a palliative in the form of the 'tally check' – a procedure which some people in fact still use. They may, for instance, be going through a list and may need to record how many times a particular event has occurred. In that case they start with individual tallies, but when the event has occurred four times instead of putting a fifth tally they put a line through the existing four. After the counting is complete the end product might, for example, be:

$$\cancel{||||} \quad \cancel{||||} \quad \cancel{||||}$$
$$\cancel{||||} \quad \cancel{||||} \quad //$$

Because counting in fives is easy very little effort is needed to determine the number involved, which in this case can be transcribed as '27'. Within the appropriate range of numbers the procedure is less laborious than using single tallies but there are similar disadvantages when the numbers become very large.

Some pupils may find it interesting to be told about the Roman notation. This involves the use of what are in effect tallies for the first three numbers, I, II, and III (and occasionally – on grandfather clocks – IIII); thereafter a number of different symbols are used – 'V' for '5', 'X' for '10', 'L' for '50', 'C' for '100', 'D' for '500' and 'M' for '1,000'. An advantage of this system is that there is no need to use more than three of the same symbol for any one number. Thus we need 'III', 'XXX', and 'CCC' for three units, tens, and hundreds; but when one more unit, ten, or hundred is added, there is the convention that a symbol to the left of another can mean that the one on the left is that much *less* than the one on the right; thus '4' is written as 'IV', '40' as 'XL', '90' as 'XC', and so on. By this means numbers up to several thousand can in principle be symbolized, and if a new symbol were invented for 5,000 it would be possible to go even higher. Long multiplication and division, however, are far easier with the Arabic notation, and the Romans would have had to devise a different notation if it had been necessary for them to deal with the very large and very small numbers that are needed in modern science.

MORE USES FOR THE NUMBER SYSTEM

One of the most ingenious devices in our present notation is the symbol '0'. In introducing it I usually say that if *all* the 'units' are taken away there are *none* left. Instead of using any of the other numerals, as we would if there were, say, four, two or one 'units' (symbolized as '4', '2', and '1'), we symbolize this situation by the use of '0'. The corresponding words are 'no' (as in the expression 'no cats in the house'), 'none' (as in 'there are none left'), and 'nought' and 'zero', which are the spoken equivalents of the symbol '0'.

The zero becomes of particular importance in the case of numbers larger than 9. Thus instead of 10 separate 'units' it is possible to substitute a single 'long'. Here the symbolization represents the number of 'longs' and the number of 'units'. Then, instead of *no* 'units' additional to the 'long', one can place one, two, or more 'units' next to the 'long'; the names are 'eleven', 'twelve', 'thirteen', and so on, and the notation is '11', '12', '13', and so on. This is a more economical way of doing things than having eleven, twelve, or thirteen 'units', all of which have to be counted.

The numbers between ten and twenty are tiresome in that, when they are spoken, information about the units comes first and information about the tens comes second, whereas in the case of the twenties, the thirties, and so on, it is the other way round. It would be less complicated for dyslexics – as well as being more logical – if convention allowed us to say 'onety one', 'onety two', and so on, but unfortunately this is not the case. There are, of course, similar complications in other languages: thus in French 'dix-sept', 'dix-huit', and 'dix-neuf' are logical, as are 'vingt-deux', 'vingt-trois', and so on, but there seems no logic in 'vingt et un' (why the 'et'?) nor in 'quatrevingts', unless it be that 'huitante' would be difficult to say. If these conventions can be 'caught' (as happens in the case of the non-dyslexic native speaker) they are unlikely to present any major difficulty. In the case of a dyslexic, however, to require him to understand the number system of a foreign language is to superimpose one very difficult task upon another!

There is a further complication in that the number of 'longs' is in fact written on the left and the number of units on the right. Now since dyslexics regularly have left–right difficulties one might be tempted to try to forestall future trouble by instructing them to put the tens on the left. It is quite possible, however, to *place* the 'long' in the right place next to the 'units' and indicate simply that that is the order in which the pupil must write numerals; and if one verbalizes at all one can simply use the expression 'next to'. Only if the pupil goes wrong or shows signs of confusion should one introduce the words 'left' and 'right'. In that case the question of a mnemonic should of course be discussed, for instance that the 'longs' are on the same side of his body as that on which he wears his watch. This, however, seems to be one of those occasions when one should not meet trouble half way; and there is no point in saddling him with a mnemonic or with confusing references to 'left' and 'right' if he does not need them.

Once the idea of so-many 'longs' and so-many 'units' is understood, the structured materials can be used in the standard way to illustrate the idea of smaller and larger numbers. For instance one might start with a 'long' and lay one, two, three, and so on, 'units' next to it, after which one might ask the pupil to say the name of the corresponding number – 'eleven', 'twelve', and so on. The procedure can then be repeated with two 'longs', three 'longs', and so on, with the pupil saying 'twenty-one', 'thirty-seven', and so on, and writing the corresponding numerals until he understands the significance of all numbers work between 0 and 100. It is also a wise precaution in the case of the written numerals to ask him, 'Which number is larger?' and 'Which number is smaller?', and to allow him, if he is in any doubt, to check against the numbers of 'longs' and 'units'. Of course once the basic principle has been grasped it becomes tedious if one carries on exercises of this kind for too long; and instead of asking the same kind of question many times over it may be preferable simply to remind the pupil that he is now permanently in a position to represent any number between 1 and 100 both by expressing it using the structured materials and by writing it.

Next one can pass to the concept of 'trading'. By this stage the pupil will be aware that ten 'units' occupy the same space as one 'long', and he will be ready to recognize the idea that ten 'units' are *equivalent* to one 'long'. Once this word is familiar, wider generalization is possible. Thus coins can be introduced, and the pupil can be shown that use of the word 'equivalence' does not necessarily mean that the objects occupy the same space, as they do when ten 'units' are equivalent to one 'long'; the issue is whether two sets of objects are of equal value – whether one set can be exchanged or 'traded' for another. Thus a 10p piece is equivalent to ten single pence in the sense of 'having the same value', an expression which they will have already met in connection with the '=' sign and of which they can now be reminded.

The way is now prepared for the teaching of 'decomposition' – in this case the breaking down of one unit in the tens column to ten units in the units column. A familiar example is that of giving change. Thus if John goes into a shop and buys something worth 16p and hands over two 10p coins he has to be given change. From what has gone before the pupil will be aware that instead of a 10p coin John could have handed over ten single pence. It is plain, however, that if 16p is needed in all a 10p piece and six single pence will be sufficient, and John will therefore have four single pence left. The pupil can then be asked to write down in numerical form what has been happening. The number of 10p pieces is written on the left, the number of single pence on the right, just as was done with 'longs' and 'units'. What John handed over was two 10p coins and no 1p coins; the correct notation is therefore '20p'. The next task is to work out what is left in the case of an object costing 16p. Clearly what we need to know is the *difference* between 20 and 16. We therefore write what we are doing in the form of a 'take-away' sum:

$$
\begin{array}{r}
20 \\
-16 \\
\hline
\end{array}
$$

Now it is very easy to take for granted that at this point no further explanation is needed – and in the case of a non-dyslexic this may well be right. Without any effort he is able to say: 'Six from nought – it can't be done; make it six from ten, which is four; change the two to a one – then one minus one is none, so the answer is four.' For the dyslexic, however, life is not so easy. Quite apart from the problem, mentioned above, of having to sort out 'left' and 'right' he may wonder whether to subtract the six from the nought or vice versa, and the 'number fact' that 'ten take away six is four' may not be immediately available to him. If he has experienced the actual operation of taking away, using structured materials, he will be aware of the *reasons* for what he is doing: he will therefore be able to work out what must be subtracted from what, and if he does not have the correct 'number fact' instantly available a small amount of counting is all that is needed.

The next stage is to show him that ten 'longs' occupy the same space as one 'flat'. This is simply a logical extension of what he has been doing. The words for the numbers are 'one hundred', 'two hundred', and so on; and he is unlikely to have any difficulty in replying with the correct number if he is given, say, three 'flats', five 'longs', and six 'units'. Similarly ten 'longs' can be traded for one 'flat'. As far as the notation is concerned, what is needed is an extra column; this enables us to record, from left to right, the number of 'flats', the number of 'longs', and the number of 'units'. It is important at this point to call his attention to the notation for writing numbers such as a hundred and seven, which involve one 'flat', *no* 'longs' and seven 'units'. Once he understands the function of the symbol '0' there will be no danger of his writing a hundred and seven as '1,007'.

Similarly 'one thousand' is represented by a 'block', 'two thousand' by two blocks, and so on. It can then be seen that 'two thousand three hundred and fifty-four' could be set out as two 'blocks', three 'flats', five 'longs', and four 'units'. As a check on whether he has understood what is happening the pupil could be asked to say the number 'a thousand and one' and then, as a difficult challenge, to write it down.

ALGEBRA

The same groundwork can also be used in introducing the pupil to algebra. Thus, to return to John and his purchase costing 16p, one might redescribe the situation as:

$$20 - 16 = \text{what?} \quad \text{or} \quad \text{What} = 20 - 16?$$

It can then be explained that we sometimes need symbols which in effect mean 'whatever number it is', without a particular number being specified. For this purpose we commonly use the symbol 'x'. Thus we might write:

$$x = 20 - 16$$

If it is considered helpful, structured materials can again be used – this time for the purpose of demonstrating equations. Represent 16 by one 'long' and six 'units' and check how many additional units are needed to make the length equivalent to two 'longs'.

It can also be explained that if we need two different 'unknowns' it is conventional to introduce 'y' as well as 'x'. Other letters are also used sometimes – common pairs being 'a' and 'b', 'p' and 'q', and 'm' and 'n'. It is probably wise to introduce these new symbols gradually and perhaps even to encourage the pupil to choose the one which he prefers.

It may also help if one points out that some symbols have more than one function. For example one use for the letters 'a' and 'b' is to represent the sounds of speech, but their function in algebra is different and their function in musical notation (where capital letters are used) is different yet again.

Earlier in the book (p. 62) it was pointed out that one can illustrate $(a + b)^2$ in the form of two-dimensional geometry. With concrete materials one can do the same thing in three dimensions. Some advanced pupils may like, in this context, to be introduced to the binomial theorem. Besides $(a + b)^2$ it may be interesting to explore $(a + b)^3$, which expands to $a^3 + 3a^2b + 3b^2a + b^3$.

Suppose we have a length a cm. and another length b cm, and for purposes of argument let us suppose that $a = 2$ and $b = 1$. Now let the pupil construct or imagine a cube $2 \times 2 \times 2$ cm, and another cube $1 \times 1 \times 1$ cm. Since $2 + 1 = 3$, and $3 \times 3 \times 3 = 27$ we need to ask how this 27 is to be made up. There has to be one cube a by a by a, that is, $2 \times 2 \times 2$ cm, and another cube b by b by b, that is, 1 by 1 by 1 cm. There also need to be three blocks of a by a by b and three blocks of b by b by a – in our example $a \times a \times a$ is $2 \times 2 \times 2$ cubic centimetres ($= 8$ cc), and

$b \times b \times b$ is $1 \times 1 \times 1$ which is 1 cc. Three blocks of a by a by b is 4×3, that is, 12; three blocks of b by b by a is 2×3, that is, 6. So the 27 is made up of $8 + 12 + 6 + 1$. Many dyslexics may prefer to think of the situation in terms of three dimensions (blocks) in place of having to deal with a series of complicated numbers or symbols. Figure 6.1 sets out the $8 + 12 + 6 + 1$, which, if suitably put together, forms a cube of $3 \times 3 \times 3$ blocks.

Some pupils may also find it interesting to discuss n-dimensional space and our limitations in being able to imagine only three dimensions, even though we can theoretically conceive of any number of dimensions.

Students may find it interesting if one discusses the job done by the word 'any'. This word behaves, in effect, like a kind of blank space. The pupil will already have learned – at least implicitly – that a number word such as 'four' can apply to *any* collection of four objects. One can therefore write a '4', followed by a blank space, and this space can then be filled in as 'four tennis balls', 'four bars of chocolate', and so on. We next have to consider the situation where the blank space has to be filled by a number, for example in the sentence, 'Give me ___ apples'. In place of the blank space we can write *any* number, whether 'three', 'five', or any other. In algebra, in place of the blank space, it is conventional to use letters of the alphabet such as 'x' and 'y', but the principle is the same. There is also a link with the English word 'whatever', since the blank or the 'x' signify '*whatever* number you choose to insert'. If necessary the pupil can be reminded of the same point when he comes to do geometry and trigonometry, where the symbol θ means 'the size of the angle *whatever* size that may be'. It should also be made clear that symbols such as 'x' and 'θ' retain the same value within the context of a given problem but that if there is a second problem they will almost certainly not have the same value as they had in the first problem. It is therefore important that the pupil should be completely clear where one sum has ended and the next one has begun. In a sense, of course, it is misleading to think of x as *any* number, since it is no different from 1, 2, 3, and so on, in having a definite value; the point is rather that until we have done some calculation we may not know what that value is.

INDICES

It is also possible to use structured materials for the teaching of indices. Again one can start with a spatial demonstration: the pupil can be asked to think of a 'long' as the side of a field and then to imagine that it is a square field. It will then be clear that a hundred 'units' take up the same space as

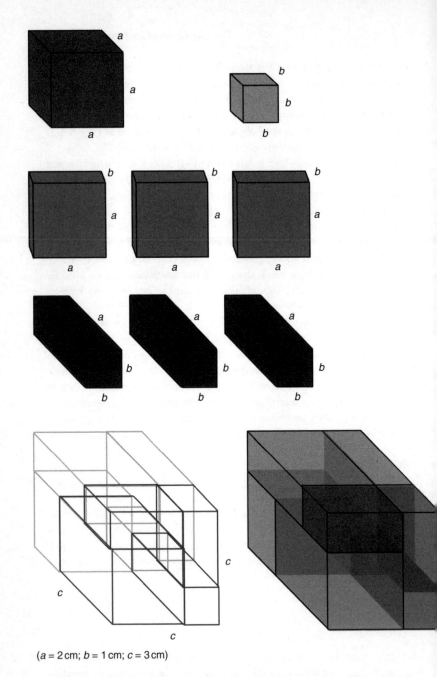

$(a = 2\,\text{cm};\ b = 1\,\text{cm};\ c = 3\,\text{cm})$

Figure 6.1 Demonstration in three dimensions of the binomial expansion $(a + b)^3$, which is equivalent to $a^3 + 3a^2b + 3b^2a + b^3$. These shapes, when fitted together, will combine to form a cube $3 \times 3 \times 3$ cm

ten 'longs' or as one 'flat'. This, too, can be expressed in symbolism:

$$1 \times 100 = 100 \text{ (this refers to the hundred 'units')}$$
$$10 \times 10 \;\; = 100 \text{ (this refers to the ten 'longs')}$$
$$100 \times 1 \;\;\; = 100 \text{ (this refers to the one 'flat')}$$

It is of course important to give the pupil time to absorb this notation and to check that he has understood it. If he has, then the teacher can say – encouragingly, as a challenge, but not minimizing the difficulty – 'You are now ready to understand a new symbol – one which we write not *on* the line but just above it.' It can then be explained that the following expressions are equivalent: 10×10 (written), 10^2 (written), 'ten squared' (spoken) and 'ten to the power of two' (spoken). When this has been made clear, the pupil can be presented with one of the written versions and asked for the spoken version, or be given the spoken version and asked to write down one or both of the written versions.

Similarly other numbers besides 10 can have squares. Structured materials can again demonstrate this. Thus there might be a square each side of which was 2 'units', in which case 4 'units' are needed to make it up. The appropriate notations are:

$$2 \times 2 = 4$$

or

$$2^2 = 4$$

Similarly the same holds of:

$$3 \times 3 = 9$$

and

$$3^2 = 9$$

and indeed will hold of any number.

When the notion of a number's 'square' has been grasped one can pass on to the notion of its 'cube'. This, too, can be represented spatially by means of structured materials. What we call 'two cubed' requires 8 'units' and what we call 'three cubed' requires 27 'units' (or 2 'longs' and 7 'units'). The notations are:

$$2 \times 2 \times 2 = 8$$

and

$$2^3 = 8$$

and

$$3 \times 3 \times 3 = 27$$

and

$$3^3 = 27$$

At a suitable point it can be explained that the small 2 or the small 3 above a number is called an 'index' figure and that index figures can be of any size. Thus:

$$10^1 = 10$$
$$10^2 = 100$$
$$10^3 = 1,000$$
$$10^4 = 10,000$$

and so on. Although a number 'squared' is a good way to lead in to the notion of an index figure, it is important to give the pupil a variety of experiences; otherwise he may make incorrect (and sometimes restricted) generalizations, for example, that an index figure is a 'little 2'.

Once indices are understood it can be pointed out how economically one can refer to very high numbers. Thus although 'a hundred million' can in principle be written as 100,000,000 it is very much easier to write it as 10^8.

The next stage is to explore some further properties of indices. The pupil will already know that ten is ten to the power of one, that a hundred is ten to the power of two, and that ten times a hundred is a thousand. We may therefore write:

$$10^1 \times 10^2 = 1,000$$

Now this is 10^3 or 10^{1+2}. In other words, in order to multiply we have *added* the index figures. Similarly:

$$10^3 \div 10^2 = 10^1 = 10$$

But 10^1 is the same as 10^{3-2}; thus in dividing we have *subtracted* one index figure from the other.

Now this is true not merely of the index figures 3, 2, and 1, but of any other index figure and bases other than ten. Thus if we use the symbol '*a*' for the base, and the symbols '*m*' and '*n*' for the indices, it is true in general that:

$$a^m \times a^n = a^{m+n}$$

and

$$a^m \div a^n = a^{m-n}$$

Once this point is clear it can be seen that there is a reason for the apparently puzzling statement that:

$$10^0 = 1$$

The pattern displayed above, in which the successive powers of 10 were shown, can now be added to. As we move up the page we read 10^4, 10^3, 10^2, 10^1. If we were to move one more step in the same direction the pattern would look like this:

$$10^0 = 1$$
$$10^1 = 10$$
$$10^2 = 100$$
$$10^3 = 1,000$$
$$10^4 = 10,000$$

It can also be made clear that these considerations do not apply only to the number 10. Any number to the power of nought is one, or, in symbols:

$$x^0 = 1$$

Now an interesting consequence of this is that in the case of numbers below one the index figure has to be negative. This point, too, can be linked to things with which the pupil is already familiar. He can be reminded of his knowledge of fractions and decimals, and in particular that, since ten 'units' make up a 'long,' a 'unit' is one-tenth, or 0.1, of a 'long'. It will not be difficult for him to think of a 'unit' being itself divisible into ten parts;

and if a 'long' (equivalent to 10 'units') had to be divided into a hundred parts each part would then have to be one-tenth of a 'unit' in length. Similarly a 'flat' might be divided into a thousand parts, and again each part would have to be one-tenth of a 'unit' in length. Since division is represented by subtraction of indices these operations can be symbolized as follows:

$$100 \div 10 = 10 \text{ or } 10^{2-1} \text{ or } 10^1$$
$$10 \div 10 = 1 \text{ or } 10^{1-1} \text{ or } 10^0$$
$$1 \div 10 = 0.1 \text{ or } 10^{0-1} \text{ or } 10^{-1}$$

Thus ten to the power of minus one is one tenth, and in general 10^{-x} is equal to:

$$\frac{1}{10^x}$$

Just as the index notation was seen to be helpful in the case of very high numbers, so also it can be helpful in the case of very low numbers. It is easier to write:

$$10^{-6}$$

than to write:

$$\frac{1}{1,000,000}$$

There can now be a further addition to our table showing the successive powers of ten. After 3, 2, 1, and nought the next number in the series must clearly be -1. The table – which can be extended as far as one wishes in either direction – now looks like this:

$$10^{-1} = 0.1$$
$$10^0 = 1.0$$
$$10^1 = 10.0$$
$$10^2 = 100.0$$
$$10^3 = 1,000.0$$
$$10^4 = 10,000.0$$

It is important to bear in mind that Dienes referred to his materials as 'multibase'; and although for many of us the important objective in the first place is to help pupils with base 10, it would be possible, if we wished, to construct materials in which the 'units', 'longs', 'flats', and 'blocks' represented a different base; for example, if we wished, like Dienes, to introduce the pupil to base 4 we would need to make a 'long' the same size as four 'units' and a 'flat' the same size as four 'longs'. Whether we do so will of course depend on what a particular pupil needs or would find interesting.

CONCLUDING REMARKS

Dyslexics are better at 'doing' than at 'naming', and a foundation of 'doing' is essential. The great advantage of structured materials is that they ensure that 'doing' comes first and 'naming' afterwards. If the order were reversed, as, sadly, it sometimes is in existing practice, one is in effect confronting the dyslexic with a mass of bewildering symbols and technical terms while not letting him have any very clear idea of what he is supposed to do with them. Once the necessary foundations have been acquired by 'doing', however, then the abstract reasoning, the generalizations, and the discoveries – which, after all, constitute the really exciting parts of mathematics – need present him with no problem.

REFERENCE

Dienes, Z.P. (1960) *Building Up Mathematics*, London, Hutchinson Educational.

Chapter 7

The use of patterns

S.J. Chinn and J.R. Ashcroft

> A mathematician, like a painter or a poet, is a master of patterns.
>
> (Hardy 1967)

INTRODUCTION

Two of the key factors which hinder a dyslexic's progress in mathematics are poor working memory (Steeves 1983) and difficulty in learning the basic number facts, particularly the times tables (Miles 1993; Mahon *et al*. 1999). In our experience of teaching dyslexics we have observed another handicapping factor, a poor ability to generalise (Joffe 1983) and classify facts and rules in mathematics.

In this chapter we consider some of the strategies which can be used to overcome dyslexics' learning problems. These problems are, of course, exacerbated by the same lack of organisation dyslexics bring to so many other areas of their lives (Smith 1978).

In our experiences of teaching arithmetic to dyslexics, we have noticed that many of our students view mathematics (which includes arithmetic, and extends into geometry, algebra, calculus, and more) as an amorphous, disjointed mixture of facts, rules and methods. Although they can understand these parts in isolation, they frequently have difficulty in mastering the interrelationships and cross-generalisations.

Our experiences lead us to believe that dyslexics need help in extending generalisations from limited areas to these interrelationships and cross-generalisations. It is one of the benefits of mathematics that rules and operations have widespread applicability and rarely have exceptions.

A teaching scheme must acknowledge the problems of the learner (Chinn 2004), but must not compromise the structure and integrity of mathematics. We are wary of teaching gimmicks which have limited applicability and which add little, if anything, to the developing of an understanding of numbers. For example, we understand and accept that most dyslexics have great difficulty in learning the times tables. Rote learning methods, whether by music, mnemonics or finger exercises are of dubious long-term benefit for many dyslexics in that they are still prone to problems with retrieval from memory and they do not teach number skills. Strategies based on developing a sound understanding of number and the form and structure of mathematics are ultimately more effective and efficient, have wider applicability and are longer lasting.

In this chapter we advocate the use of patterns, not as the sole teaching method, but as an approach to the subject which is logical and therefore emphasises the structure of mathematics and streamlines the learning of facts. The patterns are to be used as a supporting technique additional to those regularly used by teachers.

Some dyslexics develop their own strategies to bypass memory problems, but these are not always consistent. For example, Mike, a 13-year-old dyslexic, was quite successful in mathematics at school. On the Wide Range Achievement Test (Jastak and Jastak 1978) he scored at chronological age. In the subsequent oral interview he was asked to explain how he worked out some basic addition facts:

> Q. How do you add 9 and 8?
> The answer 17 was supplied very quickly. The method was to calculate via two 8s plus 1.
>
> Q. How do you add 9 and 6?
> The answer 15 was again supplied quickly. This time the method was based on the sequence for 3, that is 9 . . . 12 . . . 15.
>
> Q. How do you add 9 and 4?
> The answer was obtained by taking a 1 from the 4 and adding it to the 9 to make 10; the remaining 3 was then added on to the 10 (easily) to make 13.

Mike's strategies were unique to each of the numbers which he added on to 9. The strategies ignored any pattern based on 9. For example, once it has been established that 9 is one less than 10, and the pattern of adding to 10 is also established, then the idea of 'taking' 1 each time to make the 9 into 10 gives a pattern. This may also be viewed as a complementary pattern to adding to 10, but then adjusting the answer to be 1 less. This strategy also encourages estimation skills.

Adding 1, 2 or even 3 can be accomplished effectively and relatively efficiently by counting and so on. This could also be used to illustrate patterns such as

$$8 + 3 = 11 \qquad 18 + 3 = 21 \qquad 28 + 3 = 31 \qquad 38 + 3 = 41$$
....

Other series can be established, such as adding 7 to numbers with a units digit of 9:

$9 + 7 = 16$ (one less than $10 + 7$)
$19 + 7 = 26$
$29 + 7 = 36$
$39 + 7 = 46$
$49 + 7 = 56$ etc.

By using this technique, one fact, developed into a pattern, produces an infinite number of facts. The generalisation is that when 7 is added to any number ending in 9, the last digit becomes a 6, and the 10s digit goes up by 1.

Patterns can be seen as sequences. Such sequences can lead to small step, success-oriented, solutions to problems. They also provide a logical momentum (i.e. the pattern will carry the student forward) to facts and concepts, making them easier to teach and learn.

For example, consider the question $-3 - 1$, to which the incorrect answers $+4$ or -2 are often given. A number line puts the numbers in sequence:

$$-5 \quad -4 \quad -3 \quad -2 \quad -1 \quad 0 \quad 1 \quad 2 \quad 3 \quad 4 \quad 5 \longrightarrow +$$

An opposite presentation puts the numbers in decreasing order:

$$5 \quad 4 \quad 3 \quad 2 \quad 1 \quad 0 \quad -1 \quad -2 \quad -3 \quad -4 \quad -5 \longrightarrow -$$

This sequence and an understanding of minus relative to the sequence (which can be part of the lesson) leads to the answer -4. The sequence can be extended to provide the answer to similar problems such as $-7 - 6$.

The use of patterns can help provide a structure and organisation in mathematics, reducing the load on memory, helping understanding and helping to develop concepts. Patterns provide motivation, since success is more likely as the logical momentum of the pattern leads the learner to the correct answer.

A key question when teaching a topic or a set of facts is 'What else are you teaching?' By teaching patterns and strategies you are teaching how numbers interrelate, how one fact can lead to another and a facility with numbers that may well reduce the ever lurking menace of mathematics anxiety.

Basic requirements: some facts which must be learnt

Although it is realistic to accept that dyslexics will have great problems in trying to learn all of the basic facts of mathematics, there are a minimum number of facts which are important to learn. The facts selected are the most 'cost effective', which means they can be extended to help with the learning or computing of many other facts. Two collections of facts and one concept are essential. They can be extended with efficient strategies, strategies which will also help in building a concept of number.

Collection of facts 1

The pupil needs to know the basic addition facts from 0 to 9. These will help the child learn and understand, for example, the fiveness of 5: its relationship to other single digit numbers, its position half way to ten, its breakdown to

$$0 + 5$$
$$1 + 4$$
$$2 + 3$$
$$3 + 2$$
$$4 + 1$$
$$5 + 0$$

and the images that may help the pupil understand what 5 is, remembering that subitising (immediate evaluation) may be a problem at the five level for some pupils and that the visual pattern for five used on playing cards may address this difficulty.

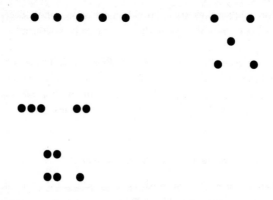

The child needs to develop a total familiarity with 5 in all its forms, for example,

5,   five,   V,   IIIII,   ĬN̶ĮI   and so on.

Collection of facts 2

The number bonds to 10 are especially important for extension work, for example, adding on to 9, or adding 8 to 16 as $16 + 4 + 4$. Again total familiarity is needed and automaticity of recall would be excellent.

Concept

In addition the pupil needs to develop an understanding of the place values of units, tens and hundreds. (The methods to be used to teach this are not described here, but should be multisensory and involve as many manipulative materials as is possible. The teacher should note the warning given later about the transfer from concrete to abstract and not assume that any particular concrete material confers the same image to the child as it does to the teacher and that different children may relate to different visual and concrete images.)

From these starting points we can develop strategies such as the pattern of adding to 9 or adding using doubles, for example;

$5 + 6$ is derived from $5 + 5 + 1$
$7 + 6$ may be derived from $7 + 3 + 3$
or from $7 + 7 - 1$
or from $6 + 6 + 1$
or from $5 + 5 + 2 + 1$

The concrete materials that may be used are Cuisenaire rods, coins, dominoes, playing cards, counters and so forth, but always the image must be linked to the symbols. Setting up flash cards for key facts may also help, and a variety of memory games can then be played with these cards.

PATTERNS IN NUMERACY – NAVIGATION THROUGH THE NUMBERS

A view of the problems

With what scheme of presentation should dyslexics be encouraged to visualise the numbers from 1 to 100?

(i) The scheme should help organisation.

(ii) The scheme should be consistent over all the numbers – all the numbers should be present in logical positions.

(iii) The scheme should unify all aspects of numeracy.

(iv) From the scheme the required extra algorithms should grow naturally.

(v) The scheme should be capable of extension to support all future work.

The way numeracy is conventionally presented is reminiscent of a railway system run by two companies – The Addition Company and The Multiplication Company. Each has its own grid of lines, but although they cross in some places no attempt is made to co-ordinate between them (clearly dangerous). The companies have (sometimes neglected) departments called Subtraction and Division, which generally have to use the same lines, but backwards and therefore prevented from seeing the signals that should help them. The Addition Company has a department called Counting, which uses lines to make very slow progress.

By contrast, we seek to show numeracy as a continuum, wherein Counting, Addition, Subtraction, Multiplication and Division grow from one another according to a structure (Figure 7.1). This structure will give support to any students, including probably the majority of dyslexics, who have unique, idiosyncratic or piece-meal understanding of numeracy, and see the distinction between the above processes (Counting, etc.) as arbitrary, to say the least.

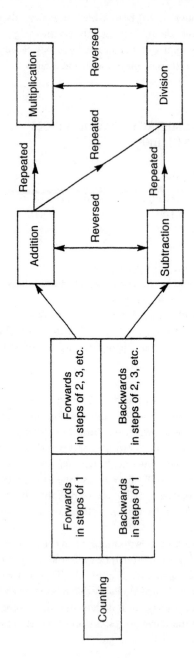

Figure 7.1 The numeracy continuum

1. When asked to subtract 5 from 8, students will often count on: 6, 7, 8 and then give the answer 3. They have reached the right answer, although they have not subtracted, but counted (or added).
2. What does the calculation '5 fours' require us to do with the 5 fours? It certainly does not require us to multiply the 5 fours together, which would give 1024! Although this calculation is usually understood to be a multiplication, it actually means 5 fours **added** together.
3. After correctly giving the answer $9 + 3 = 12$, students will sometimes explain the way they calculated it as: '9 is 3 threes and we are adding another three to give 4 threes, which are 12'. They have done the question not as an addition but as part of the easy-for-them-to-remember three times table, as we saw with Mike earlier in the chapter.
4. The question 'How many sixes are there in 42?' would usually be regarded as a division question. However, the frequently given answer that '7 sixes are 42' is the enunciation of a **multiplication** fact.

In the above illustrations, any attempt to persuade students that their selection of operation is 'wrong' would confuse and worry them unnecessarily. Perhaps the most important function of the structure developed from Figure 7.1 is to absorb all kinds of preconceptions brought to the subject by older dyslexic children. These children may have become set in their ways, the only ways they have found that work for them. The specialist teacher must find a way to build on what they know, and not seek to sweep away all that has gone before in an attempt to quickly rationalise matters, as this would imply to dyslexic children that the few things they had grasped were worthless and reinforce their fear that the subject is forever beyond them.

The authors remember seeing in a publication a statement to the effect that: 'We are now finished Addition and will move on to Subtraction – we will start again'! This approach would double the number of facts to be learned (not to mention doubling the confusion). Rather, the following examples should be seen as variations in the presentation of the same fact:

Example (i)   *Example (ii)*

$$5 + 3 = 8 \qquad 4 \times 3 = 12$$

$$5 + ? = 8 \qquad 4 \times ? = 12$$

$$? + 3 = 8 \qquad ? \times 3 = 12$$

$$5 = 8 - ? \qquad 4 = 12 \div ?$$

$$3 = 8 - ? \qquad 3 = 12 \div ?$$

Suggested solution

We suggest that a picture of the numbers 1 to 100 should be built up from a combination of patterns which will:

  (i) confirm the structure outlined in Figure 7.1,
 (ii) reveal other patterns (invaluable for streamlining learning), and
(iii) allow us to arrive at a scheme of presentation meeting our objectives for this section.

Students first learn to count in steps of 1. Unfortunately some dyslexics are unable to make much subsequent progress in numeracy. (They add by counting both numbers or by counting on from the first; they subtract by counting on or counting back: they divide by counting tally marks into groups; and so on.) Progress can be improved slowly, by counting forwards and then backwards with steps of 2, then 3, and so on, varying the starting points. Almost subliminally, counting forwards becomes adding and counting backwards becomes subtracting.

Illustrating with the number 4

The student will begin to notice that the number sequences being counted out have other patterns repeating within them. For example, within the counting 4 sequence,

$$4, 8, 12, 16, 20, 24, 28, 32, 36, 40, 44, 48, 52, 56, 60, \ldots \ldots \ldots$$

It can be seen that:

$$8 + 4 = 12$$
$$28 + 4 = 32$$
$$48 + 4 = 52$$

etc.

This confirms and reinforces another pattern consequent on the properties of adding 10s.

If these counting sequences are set out in a spiral manner, the periodic nature of the patterns becomes even more obvious:

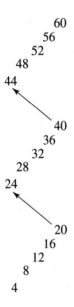

The counting 4 spiral can have different starting points, but only the first four are required to include every possible number. These are shown in Figure 7.2, followed by the spirals for 5 and 8 as further examples (see Figures 7.3, 7.4). Of these examples, the spirals for 5 repeat most rapidly, producing simple patterns which later render the 5 × table easy to learn.

The periodic nature of addition and subtraction shown in the number spiral presentation can be exploited to reduce the quantity of extra algorithms needed. In some instances, it may be possible for students to transform them into mental processes, performed with increasing rapidity, and even reaching an 'automatic' level.

Example (i)

because	$8 + 6 = 14$
then it can be understood that	$48 + 6 = 54$
and some will understand that	$48 + 36 = 54 + 30 = 84$

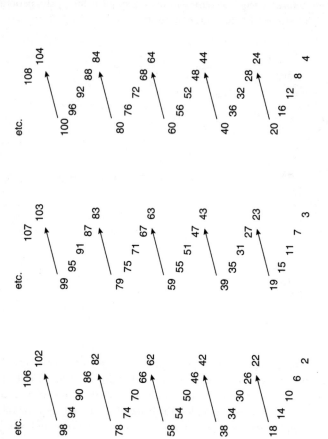

Figure 7.2 Number spirals for 4

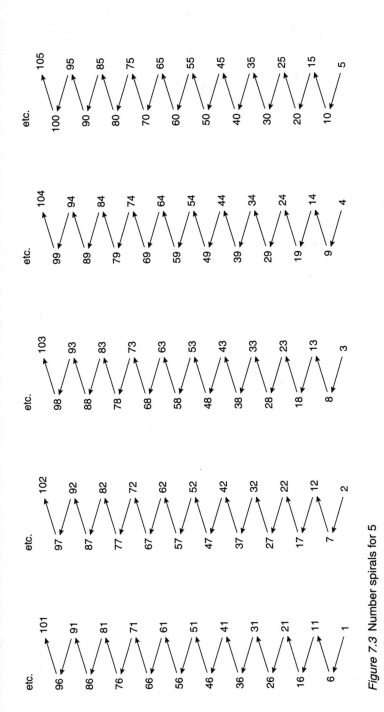

Figure 7.3 Number spirals for 5

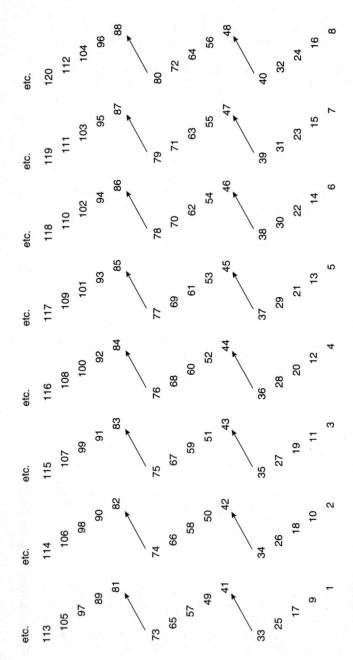

Figure 7.4 Number spirals for 8

Example (ii): some students might prefer to avoid decomposition or equal addition methods for $85 - 37$, as follows:

Because $85 - 7 = 78$

$$85 - 37 = 78 - 30 = 48$$

If all the number spirals for 4 are written adjacent to one another in vertical strings, they form a block pattern:

37	38	39	40
33	34	35	36
29	30	31	32
25	26	27	28
21	22	23	24
17	18	19	20
13	14	15	16
9	10	11	12
5	6	7	8
1	2	3	4

Read upwards, the right-hand vertical string shows the effect of adding 4 once, twice, three times, and so on, and is, therefore, the $4\times$ table. Adding has become multiplying. Read downwards, the vertical strings show the effect of subtracting 4 repeatedly and can therefore be used for divisions. For example, $28 \div 4$ (interpreted as 28 divided into 4s) is given as 7, because 28 is in the 7th row of 4s.

In fact all the operations with the number 4 (add, subtract, multiply, and divide) are summarised in the number block pattern. Consider the examples:

$$13 + 4 = 17$$
$$19 - 4 = 15$$
$$3 \times 4 = 12$$
$$28 \div 4 = 7$$
$$27 \div 4 = 6 \quad \text{remainder } 3$$

This last answer is obtainable from the block pattern: either by repeated subtraction, whereby working back from 27 leaves 3 and not another complete 4; or by repeated addition of 4s, starting with 4, which brings us to 24, with 3 remaining to reach 27.

An interesting exercise for students is to try and make all the numbers from 1 to 20, using only the number 4. This involves understanding the

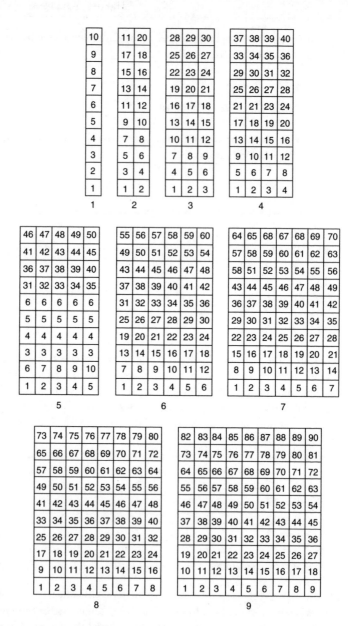

Figure 7.5 Number block patterns

91	92	93	94	95	96	97	98	99	100
81	82	83	84	85	86	87	88	89	90
71	72	73	74	75	76	77	78	79	80
61	62	63	64	65	66	67	68	69	70
51	52	53	54	55	56	57	58	59	60
41	42	43	44	45	46	47	48	49	50
31	32	33	34	35	36	37	38	39	40
21	22	23	24	25	26	27	28	29	30
11	12	13	14	15	16	17	18	19	20
1	2	3	4	5	6	7	8	9	10

Figure 7.5 continued

processes of addition, subtraction, multiplication and division, as well as the 'fourness' of 4.

$$1 = \frac{4}{4}$$

$$2 = \frac{4 + 4}{4}$$

$$3 = 4 - \frac{4}{4}$$

$$4 = 4$$

$$5 = 4 + \frac{4}{4}$$

$$6 = 4 + \frac{4 + 4}{4}$$

$$7 = 4 + 4 - \frac{4}{4}$$

$$8 = 4 + 4$$

$$\vdots$$

$$16 = 4 \times 4$$

$$\vdots$$

etc.

Figure 7.5 shows block patterns for each of the numbers 1 to 10. They can all be extended, but the block pattern for 10 takes us to the number 100 naturally and so completes the picture. Published number squares almost all proceed to the right and downwards, the way we conventionally read. However, more important in this instance is the mathematical convention that numbers increase to the right and **upwards**. This convention is adopted here, not only to maintain consistency, but also because it allows us to continue downwards below zero and into negative numbers, as outlined in part of the next section.

Further ways of using the number block patterns

1   Within our number system, the number block pattern for 10 (a 1 to 100 square) will always be the most important. A more extensive and **two-dimensional** approach can be taken to adding, where each movement to the right represents the addition of 1, while each movement upwards represents the addition of 10. For example adding thirty-two to any other number can be achieved by moving two places to the right and three places upwards. In harder cases like $49 + 25$, moving 5 units from left to right requires a jump to the line above, finishing at 54. This jump to the line above represents 'carrying' a ten, as in the written version (see below):

$$\begin{array}{r} 1 \\ 49 \\ +\ \underline{25} \\ \underline{4} \end{array}$$

2   Subtraction works in the opposite directions (downwards and to the left), but just as effectively. In harder cases like $73 - 58$, the required movement of 8 from right to left produces a jump to the line below, finishing at $\underline{65}$. In the written version, this jump represents 'borrowing' a ten and reducing the number in the tens column to $\underline{6}$ (see below):

$$\begin{array}{r} {}^{6}\!\!\!\!\!\diagup^{1} \\ \diagup\!\!\!7 3 \\ -\ \underline{58} \\ \underline{5} \end{array}$$

3   The number block pattern for 10, can be extended downwards below zero, so that similar help can be obtained in understanding addition and subtraction with negative numbers. Again, units are counted to the right

or left, while tens are counted upwards or downwards. The pattern would continue downwards, as follows:

$$-9 \quad -8 \quad -7 \quad -6 \quad -5 \quad -4 \quad -3 \quad -2 \quad -1 \quad 0$$

. . . . etc . . . . $-11 - 10$

4 Using the Distributive Law, it is possible to extend the use of the number block patterns to numbers greater than those written. It indicates, for example, that

$$9 \times 24 = 9 \times (10 + 10 + 4) = 9 \times 10 + 9 \times 10 + 9 \times 4$$
$$= 90 + 90 + 36$$

(from within the block pattern for 9)

$$= 180 + 36$$

$$= 216$$

This relates to the written method for 9×24, where we would say $9 \times 4 = 36$ and carry the 3(0), then $9 \times 2(0) = 18(0)$ and add the carried 3(0) to give 21(0).

$$\begin{array}{r} 24 \\ \times \quad 9 \\ \hline 216 \end{array}$$

5 As we have observed, the right-hand column of each block pattern represents the multiplication table for that number, and each block pattern is one column wider than its predecessor. Consequently, if the ten blocks are placed one in front of the other and joined or aligned at the left (as in Figure 7.6), the exposed right-hand columns produce a multiplication table square for 1 to 10, which can be used as such. It also remains possible to move forwards or backwards to use the block pattern on each page individually as it is needed, producing a **third dimension** of use.

Conclusion

We propose that the teaching of numeracy to dyslexics should be centred around an understanding of the above structure, based on the patterns shared by all numbers from 1 to 100.

Consequently, we propose that students should work from or refer to a set of number block patterns, rather than separate and unco-ordinated addition

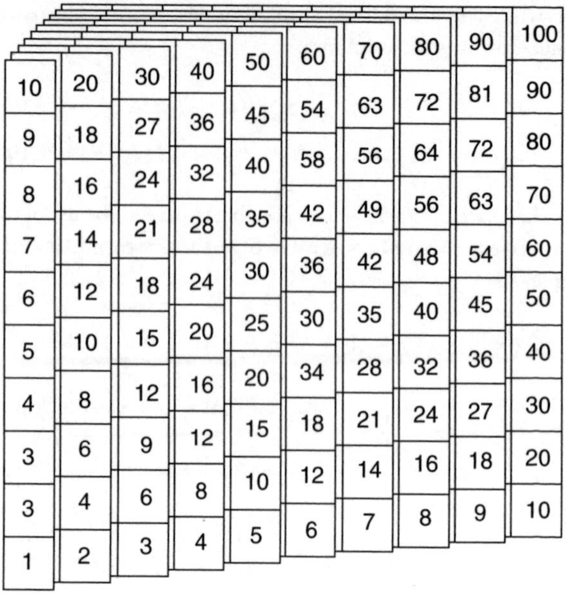

10	20	30	40	50	60	70	80	90	100
9	18	27	36	45	54	63	72	81	90
8	16	24	32	40	58	56	64	72	80
7	14	21	28	35	42	49	56	63	70
6	12	18	24	30	36	42	48	54	60
5	10	15	20	25	30	35	40	45	50
4	8	12	16	20	34	28	32	36	40
3	6	9	12	15	18	21	24	27	30
3	4	6	8	10	12	14	16	18	20
1	2	3	4	5	6	7	8	9	10

Figure 7.6 Three-dimensional effect

and multiplication tables. Since the right-hand column of each number block pattern constitutes a multiplication table, no facts are lost and the other three operations are all included. The Distributive Law is clearly demonstrated and the algorithms based upon it for longer multiplications emerge naturally.

Furthermore, any subsequent addition or subtraction sequences encountered by students will be familiar as extracts from number block patterns.

PATTERNS FOR PRACTICE AND AIDING THE ESTABLISHMENT OF CONCEPTS

The illustrations in this section are intended to reinforce other methods of teaching such concepts as multiplication of negative numbers and to provide alternative forms of practice. Their particular effectiveness for the dyslexic will be through showing that numbers of all kinds behave in a predictable, controllable and understandable way, be they whole numbers, decimals, negative numbers, fractions or algebraic terms.

There are other specific advantages:

1 *Minimal symbolism/nomenclature*
   The pattern in a number sequence obviates the need for operation symbols
   and others, which can lead to misinterpretation and ambiguity. More
   responsibility is placed on the student, from whom decision making and
   problem solving are required.

2 *Practice and understanding of the arithmetical operations*
   Most questions will require a combination of two operations, such as
   subtraction to find a difference, then addition to find the next number.
   Through checking, the reciprocity of pairs of operations will become more
   evident. Generally alternatives will be encouraged.

3 *Motivational considerations*
   Questions set as patterns or sequences are elevated into puzzles. Because of
   the choice of approaches, either directional or operational, which provides
   alternatives and the opportunity for checking, it will usually be self-
   evident when the right answer is obtained. The reassurance of success is
   invaluable.

4 *Logical momentum*
   Patterns carry a 'logical momentum'. For numbers which follow a clear
   pattern it is readily accepted that the pattern will continue, forwards or
   backwards. Students will happily allow this logical momentum to extend
   patterns into areas planned by the teacher to reinforce or help establish a
   concept.   '

Addition and subtraction sequences

For example:

$$3, 6, 9, \underline{\hspace{1em}}, 15, 18, 21, 24$$

The first step in establishing the missing number in this sequence requires
the recognition that it increases to the right by adding 3 or decreases to the
left by subtracting 3. This discovery can be made either explicitly with, for
example, a subtraction or counting on, or implicitly through a familiarity
with the numbers.

The second step is to add this 3 to 9, or subtract this 3 from 15.

Number sequences of this kind provide practice at adding and subtracting, and demonstrate the relationship between the operations and their
virtual interchangeability.

Patterns with powers

The sequence 4, 16, 64, 256, 1024, and so on, produced by multiplying successively by 4, rapidly gives numbers which are too large to manage comfortably. It provides a convincing argument for a knowledge of, and a use of, index notation, after which it becomes:

$$4^1, \ 4^2, \ 4^3, \ 4^4, \ 4^5, \ldots$$

Now another pattern is observable in the powers.

Decimal number sequences

Example: 16.0, 16.2, 16.4, __, 16.8

In this sequence, each differs from its neighbour by 0.2, or 2 in the tenths column.

Example: 2.6, 2.7, 2.8, 2.9, __, __, 3.2, 3.3

This sequence increases/decreases by 0.1. For those who might be tempted to write 2.10 for the next number, checking the sequence backwards gives:

$$2.9, \overleftarrow{3.0, 3.1, 3.2, 3.3}$$

This provides a check on the mistake, and points towards better understanding.

Example: 4.002, 4.001, ___, ___, 3.998, 3.997

In this sequence, the increase/decrease is 1 in the thousandths column, and the missing numbers straddle the awkward region:

4.000, 3.999

Again the check backwards contributes significantly.

Algebraic sequences

The following examples help to show how algebraic terms may and may not be combined.

Example: $a + 1, a + 2, a + 3,$ ___, $a + 5, a + 6$

The correct answer in this sequence is clearly $a + 4$, which confirms that the number term and the a term must be kept separate.

Example: $3a + b + 1, 3a + 2b + 1,$ _____, $3a + 4b + 1$

By obtaining $3a + 3b + 1$ for the above sequence students appreciate the need to keep separate the a, b and number terms. The convention that 1b should be written as just b is also demonstrated.

Example: $5x + y + 4, 4x + y + 6, 3x + y + 8,$ _____, $x + y + 12$

Here we are decreasing by x and increasing by 2 separately.

Division by decimals between 0 and 1

After carrying out a division such as $24 \div 0.2$, with or without a calculator, the conscientious student will check whether the answer is sensible. Most of his past experience will have shown that a number becomes smaller when divided, and the answer 120 will therefore confuse any student without a thorough understanding. The following sequence could be used instead of, or as well as, a more conventional explanation, and can be organised with or without a calculator:

$$24 \div 200 = 0.12$$
$$24 \div 20 = 1.2$$
$$24 \div 2 = 12$$
$$\text{so } 24 \div 0.2 = 120$$

Division by fractions between 0 and 1

The question $40 \div 1/2$ will very often produce the incorrect answer 20. This shows that there is only a sketchy understanding of $\div$ or that the required algorithm has been forgotten or rejected as seemingly too bizarre. Expediently, the question becomes transformed into $40 \div 2$. This incorrect version is more readily understood, requires a much simpler algorithm, or can be answered from memory. Without the repetition of a large section of work, it is difficult to convince students that the correct answer is 80, since, as previously, they expect a number to become smaller when it is divided. The following sequence is convincing, and goes some way towards explaining:

$$40 \div 8 = 5$$
$$40 \div 4 = 10$$

$40 \div 2 = 20$

$40 \div 1 = 40$

$40 \div \frac{1}{2} =$ something bigger than 40

$\qquad = 80$ (to fit in with the other answers)

$\qquad =$ the number of $\frac{1}{2}$s in 40

Multiplying directed numbers in pairs

Best established by as concrete an argument as possible, the rules can be summarized as follows:

$\qquad$ LIKE signs give $+$
$\qquad$ UNLIKE signs give $-$

$\text{or } (+a)(+b) = +ab$
$\qquad (+a)(-b) = -ab$
$\qquad (-a)(+b) = -ab$
$\qquad (-a)(-b) = +ab$

Any residual lack of understanding will be exemplified by questions such as 'How can two negatives make a positive?'

The following exercise relies on the convincing first line for its effectiveness in allowing the rules to derive themselves. (Because the following questions are in sequences, so are the answers.)

Fill in the missing answers. Put $a + $ or $-$ in each box.

$$
\left.
\begin{array}{rcl}
3 \times 5 &=& 15 \\
+3 \times\ \ +4 &=& +12 \\
(+3) \times (+3) &=& +9 \\
(+3) \times (+2) &=& +6 \\
(+3) \times (+1) &=& +3 \\
\end{array}
\right\} \quad (+a) \times (+b) = \square\, ab
$$

$$
\begin{array}{rcl}
(+3) \times\ \ 0 &=& 0 \\
(+3) \times (-1) &=& \\
(+3) \times (-2) &=& \\
(+3) \times (-3) &=& \\
\end{array}
$$

$$
\left.
\begin{array}{rcl}
(+3) \times (-4) &=& -12 \\
(+2) \times (-4) &=& -8 \\
(+1) \times (-4) &=& -4 \\
0 \times (-4) &=& 0 \\
\end{array}
\right\} \quad (+a) \times (-b) = \square\, ab
$$

$(-1) \times (-4) =$
$(-2) \times (-4) =$
$(-3) \times (-4) =$

$(-a) \times (-b) = \square\, ab$

$(-3) \times (-4) = +12$
$(-3) \times (-3) = +9$
$(-3) \times (-2) = +6$
$(-3) \times (-1) = +3$
$(-3) \times 0 = 0$
$(-3) \times (+1) =$
$(-3) \times (+2) =$
$(-3) \times (+3) =$

$(-a) \times (+b) = \square\, ab$

PATTERNS FOR GCSE

Most GCSE mathematics syllabuses contain a proportion of 'investigational' work, either as questions on examination papers or within coursework. In a large number of cases, the solutions to investigations are found by discerning the mathematical patterns beneath the surface. For example, consider a question which begins by requiring the number of matches in the tenth pattern of the following sequence:

Pattern 1   Pattern 2   Pattern 3   Pattern 4

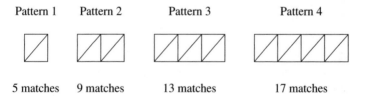

5 matches   9 matches   13 matches   17 matches

The number of matches increases by 4 from each pattern to the next. This suggests the 4 times table, but the numbers of matches are **not** the $4\times$ table. In fact the numbers 5, 9, 13, 17 are to be found in the first column of the number block pattern for 4, where the sequence starts at 1, not 4. This is because Pattern 1 contains 5 matches, one more than a multiple of 4. The answer to the question is therefore $4 \times 10 + 1 = 41$. Pattern 20 would have $4 \times 20 + 1 = 81$ matches and Pattern n would have $4n + 1$ matches.

Certain special patterns arise naturally in many different circumstances, and it is worthwhile gaining expertise in recognising and using them.

Probably the most important are:

> The even numbers 2, 4, 6, 8, 10, 12, etc.
> The odd numbers 1, 3, 5, 7, 9, 11, 13, etc.
> The square numbers 1, 4, 9, 16, 25, 36, etc.
> The triangular numbers 1, 3, 6, 10, 15, 21, 28, etc.
> The Fibonacci numbers 1, 1, 2, 3, 5, 8, 13, 21, etc.
> 2^n (1), 2, 4, 8, 16, 32, 64, etc.

Pascal's Triangle

```
              1       1
          1       2       1
      1       3       3       1
  1       4       6       4       1
1     5      10      10      5       1     etc.
```

Incidentally, as well as the combinatorial numbers, Pascal's Triangle contains the preceding three sequences, along its rows and diagonals.

In general, however, most investigations will seem to have a unique pattern, and students whose curriculum has been structured to include number pattern work will benefit from their experience.

SUMMARY

In this chapter it has been our intention to show that number patterns can help the dyslexic student in important ways. By reducing the overall number of separate facts needing to be acquired and learned, they streamline the learning process. The regularity and structure they bring to the subject compensate for the student's own lack of organisation, and enhance his ability to establish interrelationships and cross-generalisations.

The help is available at all stages of development, from the level of very basic numeracy to GCSE level. At almost every stage in between, number patterns can provide alternative forms of practice to aid conceptual development. They can be used as much or as little as the teacher sees fit, the flexibility of their applicability being one of their biggest advantages.

Finally, it should be added that the benefits gained through experience with number patterns are not confined to mathematics. As a quantitative form of generalisation, their recognition can be useful in other school subjects, such as the sciences or geography, and in areas of everyday life.

REFERENCES

Chinn, S. (2004) *The Trouble with Maths: A Practical Guide to Helping Learners with Numeracy Difficulties*, London, RoutledgeFalmer.

Hardy, G.H. (1967) *A Mathematician's Apology*, Cambridge, Cambridge University Press.

Jastak, J.F. and Jastak, S. (1978) *Wide Range Achievement Test* (revised edn), Wilmington, DE, Jastak Associates.

Joffe, L. (1983) 'Dyslexia and attainment in school mathematics . . . a matter of verbal labelling, generalisation, horses and carts', *Cambridge Journal of Education*, 13(3), 22–7.

Mahon, D., Chinn, S., Van Elswijk, R., Harmsen, H. and Kay, J. (1999) 'Comparative study of perceived difficulties in mathematics experienced by children with specific learning difficulties in Ireland, England and the Netherlands', *Irish Educational Studies*, 18, 199–209.

Miles, T.R. (1993) *Dyslexia: The Pattern of Difficulties*, London, Whurr.

Smith, S. (1978) *No Easy Answers*, Rockville, NIMH.

Steeves, J. (1983) 'Memory as a factor in the computational efficiency of dyslexic children with high abstract reasoning ability', *Annals of Dyslexia*, 33, 41–52.

Chapter 8

Steering a way through number facts

S.A. Turner Ellis

Dyslexic pupils have a difficult passage through this area. Daniel was my dyslexic pupil back in 1989, and since then our knowledge of teaching number facts to dyslexics has moved on. Today I would be able to teach Daniel more effectively by employing the practical implications of my research as well as drawing on the advice of my (dyslexic) husband, Tony who also teaches. It is these experiences that I want to share with you in this chapter. Reference is also made to a Mathematics Pack, which is a pack of blank cards written on during the course of study, with useful information that can be used as a memory jogger for the pupil.

This chapter is in five parts. The first is concerned with 'the age of the dyslexic pupil'; it emphasises the importance of the age of the pupils because this affects the rate of progress. The second, 'Barriers to overcome', illustrates the mathematical 'barriers' that dyslexics need to pass. In the third part, 'Speeding along', practical advice is given to help speed up number fact acquisition and rate of responding. In the fourth, 'Boosting confidence' – since as teachers we are in constant demand to boost flagging confidence – several teaching tips are shared. Finally, and most fascinating of all, in the penultimate section 'Seemingly redundant behaviour by dyslexics' – I present some of the observations of the behaviour of dyslexics that I made while they were doing mathematics. I ask *why* they spoke and moved so much when carrying out calculations, and what, if anything, should be done about it. The chapter ends with the section 'Overall conclusions'.

THE AGE OF THE DYSLEXIC PUPIL

Young dyslexics

I flashed some sums, for example, $24 + 8$, $68 - 5$, $56 \div 7$, 3×4, individually on a computer screen and asked Andrew, a dyslexic pupil aged 10 years, and

Robert, a non-dyslexic 10-year old, to respond by typing in their answers as quickly as possible. Some interesting things happened as a result. Andrew responded by taking about 7 seconds longer than Robert to answer each of the questions. Andrew also had far fewer number facts at his disposal and made noticeably more errors. I was interested to know if Andrew's difficulty was true of older dyslexics. On further enquiry this turned out to be the case, though less pronounced. From a teaching viewpoint, dyslexic 10-year olds appear to be at a distinct disadvantage when answering number fact questions quickly and accurately. An obvious question is to enquire about how even younger dyslexics perform in the mathematical classroom. It seems desirable to study the learning progress of young dyslexics of around 5 years of age and seek to remediate any early signs of number fact difficulties as early as possible, as is done with literacy teaching.

Age of gain

The results of my research study enabled me to discover the age at which most gains in accuracy and speed in performing sums were made. I found that the dyslexics made most noticeable progress between the ages of 10 years 7 months and 12 years 7 months, which was found to be 3 to 4 years later than a similar spurt by the non-dyslexics. These particular children were in a favourable environment with a caring atmosphere where their dyslexia was catered for, so it shows that improvement by the dyslexic is possible. The implication for teachers is that dyslexics may well take longer to learn their number facts and respond at speed and with accuracy than the majority of their classmates. The teacher may need to take appropriate measures such as reviewing number facts regularly and not putting undue pressure on the dyslexic learner to perform better when they are in fact doing the best that they can. Parents may also need reassurance and guidance. At around the age of 13 years the dyslexic may have become fairly proficient at number facts and what is important is to keep up the momentum of number fact rehearsal and usage.

Teenage dyslexics

One of the things you may like to look out for is an unexpected decline in number skills from around 14 years of age when knowledge of number facts may have become rusty. This was one of the most surprising findings in the research and leads one to question whether the number facts remain secure for the dyslexic once learned. It is possible that this rustiness causes some dyslexic teenagers to feel disheartened and unable to perform well in mathematics or even in school in general. Like a vicious cycle this can lead to stress and emotional difficulties.

Steeves (1983) recognised that dyslexics could be mathematically gifted but warned of possible dangers if help is not given:

> If the needs of gifted children are not met by appropriate program-ming in school, the resultant frustration may cause them to become under-achievers or even high school dropouts. The highly intelligent dyslexic, already an under-achiever in the area of language, becomes doubly handicapped if his or her mathematical talent is not fostered or challenged.

This talent can exist, she said, alongside a 'lack of computational efficiency'.

In order to help avoid the resultant frustration, teachers should be aware of the need to review number fact skills on a regular basis throughout the mathematical course, even if the pupil is over 13 years of age. Review of even the $1\times$, $2\times$, $3\times$, $5\times$, $10\times$, and $11\times$, tables should be made. This helps to ensure that confidence is raised by the knowledge that the foundation skills are secure. Additionally this may help to reduce both confusion with other number facts and also slowness in decision-making.

In my experience, regular review of multiplication facts is essential for confidence building and success. A student of mine some years ago received help with mathematics up to his GCSE's, and every week I encouraged him to practise his multiplication facts. There was at times some resistance, but I found that without these facts being accessible, we were unable to move through some of the topics he was learning, due to gaps in his knowledge. He was unable to recognise patterns. Long division was difficult because of his poor memory; consequently the procedure in solving the problem overwhelmed him. This situation was reversed when he had finally grasped the facts.

What about the child who simply cannot rote learn the facts? In these circumstances, the fluent use of the 12×12 multiplication grid is essential. Another student I taught found herself in this position, so we regularly practised completing the grid from scratch on a blank sheet of paper. In time she was able to complete the task within 6 minutes. She was coached to reproduce the grid during the 10-minute reading time of any exam. This enabled her to take full advantage of her ability to process problems quickly and accurately without overwhelming her memory. The need to monitor progress continually is essential: in the case of dyslexics there is extra danger that what they have learned may not be retained because they have had insufficient repetition.

BARRIERS TO OVERCOME

In mathematics there are a number of barriers. These are seen, for example, when converting from minutes into hours (the minutes/hours barrier) or when changing from pence into pounds (the pence/pounds barrier). Each number is labelled as having a particular value which needs to change according to its position. It is the extra labelling caused by these requirements that can be tricky for the dyslexic.

Crossing the ten barrier

In our base ten system new labels for numbers are required, as when counting up from 1 to 12. Here, the written representation of numerals takes account of this and the move from 9 over the ten barrier requires the mathematician to use two numbers rather than one to represent '10' and also for the numbers '11' and '12'. The meaning of the use of the numeral '12' is 'one ten and two left over', illustrating a grouping of numbers into tens.

Consider the concept of the ten barrier when subtracting. On a question like $30 - 1$ you have to change two numbers to achieve the answer of 29. This is unlike $37 - 3$ where only the number in the 'ones' position needs to change for the answer of 34. Thus the ten barrier refers to a cross over bridging changes in the 'tens' value.

Sorting out the wood from the trees

The use of manipulates such as Cuisenaire rods and Dienes blocks is essential for this concept to be understood by a dyslexic. Sally, a classroom assistant, was asked to help make exciting homemade games to help the children understand the ten barrier concept. We drew single trees to represent 'ones', single woods composed of ten trees to represent 'tens' and single forests to represent 'hundreds' or 'ten lots of tens'. Each picture was drawn in vividly coloured felt pen on card and then laminated for preservation. Roger, a 6-year-old dyslexic pupil, began Sally's game by shaking a dice. He threw a six and with a *yelp* then gathered up six individual trees. His opponent Kelly then threw a five with the dice and scooped up five trees. It was Roger's turn and this time he threw a four. He reached for four trees and counted his new total of trees. This was six plus the four new trees, making ten. He realised that he could now say, 'Please may I exchange my ten trees for one wood' (made up of ten clearly drawn trees with blossom and apples drawn beautifully by Sally). Roger then gave his trees to Sally, who acted as the 'banker', and she handed one wood to him, to his delight. Then it was Kelly's turn. Both children were keen to reach the grand target of five woods (representing fifty) and each hoped that they would be the winner.

Sally had a wonderful imagination and she thought up other ways of representing 'ones', 'tens' and 'hundreds'. 'How about houses to represent "ones," streets with ten houses and towns (with a hundred houses)?', she announced. She also whispered to me that she thought the game could be played in reverse to illustrate subtraction with borrowing. 'Why don't the children start with five woods (50) and then throw the dice and subtract by that amount, exchanging ten single trees for one of their woods (a group of ten trees) and then subtracting. The winner would be the first to have no trees left and reach zero. Sally therefore helped the children overcome the ten barrier hurdle in a way that the children could relate to in real life so that they would be 'out of the woods' and away with their mathematical understanding!

Sally's drawings were next accompanied by numerals written by the children and both Roger and Kelly enjoyed a new game of building up the numbers and their pictorial representations one by one, starting with 0, 1, 2 and placing the correct number of individual trees beside the digits, laying their work across the classroom floor in sequential order. After 9, Kelly then reached for the written number 10 and Roger shouted, 'We need one wood for that'. Kelly then realised that the number 1 in the numeral '10' meant one wood (or group of ten) and no single trees left over. 'Yes – so for 11 we need one wood and one tree'. Roger was brimming with enthusiasm at their discovery. When the children reached 20, two woods were grabbed and the children started to think big. 'What about 99?' said Roger. 'That's 9 woods and 9 trees', said Kelly. '100 must be ten woods then' she said. 'Yes and that means we need one forest instead', said Roger with triumph. He went on, 'So 100 means 1 forest, no wood and no trees left over'. The children had discovered our base ten system and were keen to share it with the rest of the class, explaining their findings in peer group language to their classmates so that it was easily understandable for them.

How would Roger have performed later on with the question '68 + 7'? Older dyslexics in my research had great difficulty in crossing quickly and accurately up into the 70s to reach the answer 75, especially when they were compared with non-dyslexics. A similarly difficult question '34 − 8' also caused comparative difficulty, because of the relabelling from the 30s into the 20s across the ten barrier. Memory for pairs of numbers that go together to make ten is invaluable knowledge for answering these questions (see Yeo 2003). To help our pupils we present 'barrier flash cards' starting with number bonds to 10 and then number bonds beyond 10. These cards have been put into the student's Mathematics Pack for review on a regular basis. They help in memory retrieval, and with practice their fluency improves. It is expected also that the 100 and 1,000 barriers will cause similar difficulties when we get to them, so the flash cards will help here too.

Hurdling the decimal point barrier

Punctuation for dyslexics poses problems. The decimal point can be likened to a full stop within mathematics. The inclusion of a decimal point in a number represents the distinction between the whole number and a fraction. The concept in base ten of numbers decreasing in value from left to right is potentially confusing. The more numbers there are after the decimal point, the smaller is the value of the right-hand number. This may appear confusing since one would imagine that a number with more digits in it would represent a large value. The difficulty with place value, that dyslexics often experience, extends to the appreciation that the decimal point represents the move into tenths, hundredths and thousandths of a number, and so on.

Money and measurement also involve the use of the decimal point and therefore a working knowledge of the 'barrier' concept is important. When children are asked the question, 'Which is more expensive – an item worth £12.99 compared with an item at £13?' encouragement is needed to appreciate that although £12.99 has more numbers in it, it does not represent a higher value (the concept of rounding would be presented at this stage).

Re-labelling in other areas

My research results call into question how familiar the dyslexic is with any mathematical situation that requires some sort of re-labelling, such as metres and kilometres, pounds and ounces, where a barrier or separator is in operation. In my experience dyslexic students find it difficult to convert from one unit to another and to appreciate the need to do so in some circumstances, in order to solve a particular problem. One example is the need to appreciate the relation between hours and minutes in base 60, as in this question:

Add:

hours	minutes
9	52
+ 6	16

My husband, Tony, had a memorable experience while on holiday in the Canary Islands. He had difficulty converting to the local currency and nearly bought a watch that was vastly over-priced, much to the delight of the shopkeeper with whom he bartered.

Such 'barriers' may be responsible for a lessening of speed and accuracy in a range of mathematical tasks and this has huge implications for our teaching priorities when helping dyslexics.

SPEEDING ALONG

The ability to use number facts at speed is a great advantage in life. Some people are fully automatic in their production of the answer to '7 × 8' for example. Some people on the other hand, including many dyslexics, find that they can't remember number facts very well and a calculator may not always be at hand or be appropriate. This could be embarrassing and cause 'hold-ups' when working out more complicated mathematical problems that require a number of steps.

Can dyslexics respond speedily?

To investigate the possibility of a dyslexic difficulty with knowing number facts at speed, I counted up the number of correct answers to sums given in less than 2 seconds. The details given here relate to 30 dyslexic boys aged 9 to 15 and 30 controls matched in relevant respects including intelligence as judged by their scores on the Children's Matrices or the Raven Standard Progressive Matrices. The questions were chosen from the four operations, for example: 6×4, $49 \div 7$, $34 + 2$, $48 - 5$. Table 8.1 shows the very interesting results and Figure 8.1 illustrates these.

From Table 8.1 and Figure 8.1 it can be seen that the dyslexics seem to be at a distinct disadvantage in their ability to answer number facts speedily. This is true for all the operations and means that dyslexics need longer to respond in the classroom and during examinations with questions that involve the use of number facts.

Practice in writing numbers to dictation both fluently and accurately

It follows from the research that dyslexics could benefit from training in increasing their fluency when working with numbers. One way to do this is to give extra practice in writing numbers down to dictation. Speedy and accurate work is the target. I have children practise writing numbers in words as part of the literacy programme I follow. Moreover, it is great fun for the child to imagine writing out a cheque in a bank for large sums of money.

Table 8.1 Number of correct responses given in under 2 seconds on each operation by the dyslexics and non-dyslexics

Operation	Group	
	Dyslexics	*Non-dyslexics*
×	884	1,678
÷	406	976
+	30	196
−	10	194
Total	1,330	3,044

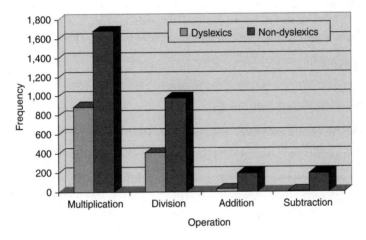

Figure 8.1 Number of correct answers given in under 2 seconds on each operation by the dyslexics and non-dyslexics

This improves their spelling of say 'million' and it gives them practice at the exercise. Reversing the process is equally important as practice is gained in place value work when changing from words to numbers.

Verbal labelling of numbers at speed

If children can articulate numbers more readily, more mental resources become available for processing the problem. Often children become shaky at saying large numbers when presented in standard form, for example,

201,084. This skill can be improved with practice and this is where a card with such a number on can be placed in the Mathematics Pack for review and reinforcement.

I found in my research that in subtraction and more particularly in addition, dyslexics were much slower when crossing the ten barrier. Dyslexics can benefit from extra experience of counting across the ten barrier as fluently as possible both forwards and backwards. The aim of the extra practice would be to help counting become more automatic, thereby enabling mental resources to be re-allocated to other aspects of the mathematical process. Often such counting skills are taken for granted in children's schooling and perhaps more attention should be given to the study and support of the dyslexic individual's counting rate and accuracy.

Experience in speed counting may be extended to include crossing the hundred, thousand, ten thousand, hundred thousand and million barriers both forwards and backwards, as well as moving into negative numbers over the zero barrier and overcoming the decimal barriers. All this would be introduced at the appropriate time for the student, with the teacher taking care to ensure earlier foundation skills are still firmly in place.

Practising number bonds to ten

The use of concrete materials helps the dyslexic student to understand the relationship between numbers that sum to ten. It doesn't take dyslexics long to realise that they can use their fingers as concrete aids, provided that they follow a familiar sequence. This, however, has the disadvantage of slowing the computation process down. It is therefore important that number bonds to ten be memorised by the inclusion of number bond cards in the Mathematics Pack – for example, a six can be written on one side of the card and four on the other side. This has been found to help in immediate recall of important facts under timed conditions. One efficient approach would be to teach facts that can be replicated in other groupings of ten, such as $42 + 8 = 50$ and $52 + 8 = 60$, where a knowledge of number bonds to ten $(2 + 8)$ proves an invaluable pattern to memorise.

Doubling and halving

Teachers of dyslexic students and dyslexic students themselves have advocated the skill of doubling and halving numbers as a way of working through to an answer. Two examples are: using $2 \times 6 = 12$ to work out 4×6 by doubling, or conversely, halving, the answer to $8 \times 8 (= 64)$ to work out 4×8. In my own teaching several students have found such skills very useful. Chris, a 15-year-old student, who has difficulties remembering some multiplication facts, relies heavily on the concept of doubling numbers to find the answer to sums such as '$6 \times 7 = 42$'. He uses $3 \times 7 = 21$, then doubles to find his answer.

BOOSTING CONFIDENCE

A child who feels confident can approach their learning with a positive frame of mind and potentially make the greatest progress. As for the teacher, the qualities of patience, sympathy and understanding can boost a child's belief in themselves. Six possible ways of developing confidence are outlined here:

(i) Observe and ask how the learner does mathematics   As Street (1976), a dyslexic learner, concluded in her own case and that of another student; they had needed 'a teacher trained to understand the way our cognitive styles differed from those of other children, and who was also trained to adapt her teaching to our needs'.

Such an approach towards the teaching of mathematics requires keen observation of small details and enquiries directed at how the child is performing their mathematics. This may sometimes be outwardly observable, but there are instances where it may not be obvious as to how the mathematics is being worked out by the child. If the teacher asks some questions, however, subsequent replies from the child may be enlightening for the teacher and also act as a confidence booster for the child whose ideas may prove to be perfectly valid.

To ask if a child is good at multiplication may be misleading since he is likely to be more accurate and quicker with some products than with others; also children may exaggerate their knowledge to avoid peer pressure or even teacher involvement. Thus in the case of all operations, the first step is to discover the areas of strength and weakness in a specific way. Such discoveries can steer the planning and implementation of remediation.

During my own research project several dyslexics became confused as to which number in a multi-digit answer to type on the computer first. When Oliver did multiplication sums he liked to check the screen to see if his answer had been typed in correctly. Similarly Alex said, 'I tend to get numbers the wrong way around', for example, $2 \times 8 = 61$, $6 \times 2 = 21$, $7 \times 2 = 41$, $2 \times 9 = 81$. For $1 \times 11 = 11$ Alex said, 'I could hardly get that one back to front!' He searched for the keyboard numbers and then checked up on the screen to see if the numbers had been typed in correctly, which was quite a demanding task for him.

Speed of answering could be delayed because of confusion with the operation required, for example, Robert (doing multiplication) was observed to say and do the following: 'It's gone . . . I just had it . . . I keep thinking it's divide'. When he had to respond to 5 × 5 he said, 'Is ten I think' and then used his fingers to arrive at the answer 25. The multiplication sign had been confused with an addition sign.

These observations point to the need for teachers to draw attention to the identifying 'features' of each sign representing the four operations, to help build meaningful associations. Reinforcement may be achieved through including symbol cards and numbers in the Mathematics Pack. It is also worthwhile finding out how a dyslexic works out a problem in order to help them become more efficient; interest shown in their approach also gives them confidence.

(ii) Link to current interests – pupils' own ideas for reminders Considerable over-learning of number facts is needed. In my own teaching I find that dyslexics respond best when knowledge is linked to current interests, such as 'Harry Potter', especially when the ideas are generated by the pupils themselves. Adam, my Year 7 pupil, developed an idea for learning multiplication tables. Adam used his lively imagination and thought of a way to link the multiplier and product on either side of each step in Harry Potter's staircase (Rowling 1997). Harry was forced to have his bedroom under the stairs. We began by choosing a multiplication table to revise, such as the 7 times table. Adam drew twelve steps and I proceeded to place the numbers from 1 to 12 under each step (see Figure 8.2). These represented the multipliers. Adam then filled in the product on each step above the correct multiplier in a different colour. He then studied the numbers for any patterns and drew in arrows to show these. Such a topical approach enlivened many a lesson and provided enjoyment, creativity and a lasting association to be formed for the number facts.

Charlotte, an American pupil in Grade 3, made thematic posters of difficult multiplication tables (60 cm × 90 cm), which she displayed on her bedroom walls. Charlotte took great care in producing the colourful posters, and she incorporated many of her own thoughts, enabling her to build a relationship with the number facts in a unique way.

Jessica even placed number fact cards around her house, such as in the fridge, behind the bathroom door, on the television, in the car – so that she could revise the facts on a regular basis. Jessica found that she preferred to concentrate on a few key number facts each week. Her repertoire soon built and her parents were able to quiz her on the relevant facts that she had chosen for that week.

(iii) Teach the easy number facts first – using mnemonics for the most challenging number facts Multiplication facts contribute significantly to the

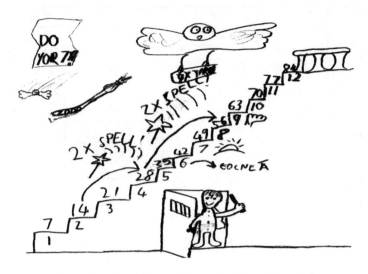

Figure 8.2 Harry Potter's staircase (drawn by Adam Kelvey)

mathematical operations children are taught in the teenage age group. Topics such as fractions, percentages, area, volume, Pythagoras, square numbers, prime factors, algebra, factorisation to name but a few, all rely on the often-instantaneous response to multiplication facts. Alternatively, patterns involving the facts, for example, the 5× table, used to read the minute hand on clocks, can appear anywhere, which when recognised can give confidence to children in solving problems.

It makes sense that we teach the tables with obvious regularities (Henderson and Miles 2001). These are the tables that dyslexics feel most successful with. It is helpful initially to learn the number facts that are easier to acquire, in order to encourage and promote confidence. My research showed that these number facts were the 1, 2, 3, 5 and 10 multiplication and division tables, especially with low multipliers and quotients. Often dyslexics learn through hearing a pattern such as in the 10 times table or the sequence of the 5 times table. By asking children to fill in the multiplication grid with the easier tables, in the two directions of the grid, much of it becomes completed, leaving very few facts left to do. This is illustrated in Figure 8.3. This simple presentation to a dyslexic student can often show the manageability of the task. Thus confidence to observe patterns grows. The grey shaded area in the diagram represents the most difficult number facts for dyslexics, and Jack, my pupil, called this the 'Titanic Iceberg' area; it is perfect for the use of memory joggers.

×	1	2	3	4	5	6	7	8	9	10
1	1	2	3	4	5	6	7	8	9	10
2	2	4	6	8	10	12	14	16	18	20
3	3	6	9	12	15	18	21	24	27	30
4	4	8	12		20					40
5	5	10	15	20	25	30	35	40	45	50
6	6	12	18		30					60
7	7	14	21		35					70
8	8	16	24		40					80
9	9	18	27		45					90
10	10	20	30	40	50	60	70	80	90	100

Figure 8.3 Multiplication grid with the 'Titanic Iceberg' area (in grey)

It is well known within the field of special needs, that if a child can make *personal* associations and develop their *own* mnemonics then their memory for the knowledge is more secure. Examples of helpful mnemonics are: for '7 × 7' – 'Wakey, wakey rise and shine 7 × 7 is 49!' After giving some as examples, get the pupil to think up some more. Helping the child build on a repertoire of associations in a fun way can be very effective, especially for the more challenging multiplication facts such as: 6 × 6, 7 × 6, 8 × 6, 7 × 7, 7 × 8 and 8 × 8. The more imaginative and bizarre the mnemonics the greater the appeal and the more memorable they become.

Once some key facts have been memorised these can act as 'anchor points' and be used to work out other unknown facts surrounding them, thereby reducing 'working out' time. Daniel, a dyslexic 12-year old tackled the question '8 × 9' using his anchor point of 81 as follows: 'At first nothing came into my head, and then I remembered 9 × 9 = 81 and subtracted'.

Vigilance is needed to spot habitual errors that occur in the children's calculations, especially at the outset. It was noted that Nicholas (doing a multiplication sum) made an error in his counting up of the 5 times table as follows: '5 × 5' was worked out on his fingers as '5, 10, 15, 25, 30' and so he gave the answer as 30. Likewise '8 × 5' was again calculated, using fingers, as '5, 10, 15, 25, 30, 35, 40, 45' and he came to the answer 45. In both instances he had omitted 20. I have noted in my teaching career that an error committed in the first instance tends to recur consistently and become a habit if not addressed. My advice is to take up these errors early.

(iv) Recognising the interrelationship of the four operations   Dyslexic children often translate from one operation to another between the four operations in order to solve mathematical problems. They use whatever compensatory strategies they have developed for themselves. One of these might be to use a known number fact, for example, '6 × 3 = 18' to work out an answer in another operation such as '18 ÷ 3'. This may be thought of as either 'how many 3s make 18?' or '3 times what number equals 18?'. This knowledge is sophisticated and shows that dyslexics are capable of understanding quite complex relationships between numbers. Arthur translated a division question into a multiplication question by counting up in 2s to find the answer to 14 ÷ 2, and similarly Robert said, '11 times something . . .' in response to the question 88 ÷ 11.

Dyslexics are also adept at 'compensating' by converting an addition or subtraction question into an easier question by temporarily adding or subtracting a smaller number. This approach involves being on the lookout for an easier calculation than the one set. For example, Andrew used addition in a subtraction sum, when working out 51 − 28, by adding 28 + 2 (30), then adding 20 and then 1. He had added 2 + 20 + 1 to give the correct answer 23.

Such strategies have the advantage of increasing the pupil's repertoire of number facts. This approach, though slow and laborious by an outsider, is often the only strategy that will allow the dyslexic to achieve success, particularly under examination type conditions; this is why the need for extra time is warranted.

It is desirable to teach the commutative property of multiplication (*a* × *b* = *b* × *a*) early in the training, and to give it regular revision, thereby reducing the number of facts needed to be memorised. Similarly the dyslexic finds it a help if he realises that there is a commutative property for addition too so that, like multiplication, it can be done in any order (e.g. 5 + 2 gives the same answer as 2 + 5). It is important to make it absolutely clear that the commutative property does not hold for subtraction or division since, for example, 28 − 4 is not the same as 4 − 28 (−24), nor is 42 ÷ 7 (6) the same as 7 ÷ 42!

Other relationships can be shared too. A knowledge that subtraction is the inverse operation of addition, that multiplication can be thought of as repeated addition and that division is like repeated subtraction gives the dyslexic child a greater range of compensatory strategies.

(v) Avoiding fast talk − 'My mind is full up'   Again and again research has shown that dyslexics are not as readily able to cope with a fast rate of delivery by their instructors. The teaching plan, therefore, should include plenty of time for absorption of learning, with less 'fast talk' by the teacher,

but slower delivery that includes carefully chosen key words and phrases. Street (1976) wrote of the importance of specificity of words in instruction and explained in her own case that 'the more difficult she (the teacher) saw that I was finding the sum, the more words she produced', which served to confuse her further.

Daniel, a dyslexic 10-year old, was typing in his answers to timed multiplication sums that were flashed on a computer screen in front of him. He announced that his mind was 'full up' and that he found it hard to move on to the next question. There was a long pause while he recovered. This response from Daniel indicated that he was prone (like many dyslexics) to memory overload, especially when under the pressure of time. Dyslexics can become completely unable to absorb information in these circumstances and therefore teachers need to give them time to recover rather than become overwhelmed with more information.

(vi) Ability at mathematics – fingers are a start   Just because a dyslexic child has difficulty remembering number facts and maybe uses his fingers, this should not perpetuate the notion that he is not able to pursue the subject to a higher level. Indeed Jansons (1988) is one example of a dyslexic who has succeeded in mathematics despite such difficulties. He gained a place at King's College, Cambridge to read mathematics, obtained a distinction and then undertook a PhD in fluid mechanics. He went on to become a lecturer in mathematics at University College London. Jansons might not have followed this path were it not for his teacher, who had recognised his talents and given him encouragement. It follows that dyslexics need sympathetic and observant teaching to promote their abilities and raise their confidence in a subject that they may have potential for.

SEEMINGLY REDUNDANT BEHAVIOUR BY DYSLEXICS

It is interesting that many years ago MacMeeken (1939) referred to the importance of observing 'how' children with educational difficulties performed tasks. She noted the intense effort displayed, saying; 'Such effort is in many cases accompanied by exaggerated tongue and lip movements, movements of the head, facial grimaces, even by other body movements, say, of arm or leg.'

In the course of my teaching I have noticed that dyslexics often fidget with their hands when they are in a listening situation in class. Also during the research it became apparent that the dyslexic children were behaving differently from their non-dyslexic peers when carrying out mathematical work. They displayed a great deal more physical movement and muttering than I had expected and certainly much more than the non-dyslexics.

Here are some of the interesting movements made by the dyslexics while they were doing the mathematical tasks: frequent use of their fingers to work out the problem, toes feeling the curve of the table leg, scratching itches on the neck and wrists, waving hands above the key board, running fingers through a fringe, adjusting glasses, sniffing, rolling up sleeves, rubbing the nose after every answer, and rhythmically tapping a foot. In addition to this, much was said, such as: echoing the question, working out loud, giving comments and observations about the experiment, giving big sighs, and comments of exasperation. It was as though their thinking had to be carried out overtly.

Here are some of the actual words that were spoken by different dyslexics:

- 'Its gone. I just had it' (an example of a dyslexic trying to hold on to a thought – trying to remember it).
- 'Oh bother'.
- 'I'm rushed. If I had more time I could work it out . . . I get muddled up'.
- On seeing the question $108 \div 9$, the pupil choked jokingly (indicating that this question was hard for him).
- 'I hate division' (said very sweetly), big inhalation with a difficult question as though working up to making a decision.
- 'Come on!' (Showing the intent of the dyslexic participant to do as well as possible – with self-inflicted pressurisation.)
- 'I am reacting too soon – jumping the gun – and pressing the wrong keys because of it.'
- 'I am slow at thinking' (indicating that the dyslexic was aware of their slow processing of mathematical information).
- $10 \times 11 = 100$. 'I want 110. Oh flip', $11 \times 10 = 101$ 'Oh, I've done it again, 110 again,' $10 \times 10 = 110$ 'This time'; $10 \times 2 = 10$ 'Oh no, 20'; $11 \times 10 = 100$, 'Oh no, 110'; $2 \times 2 = 2$, 'Oh no, it's 4'.
- $1 \times 11 = 11$ 'I could hardly get that one back to front!'
- 'My mind is full up' – here the dyslexic came to a standstill, and found it hard to move on to the next question (indicating that the dyslexic brain became overloaded, and could not continue to function until it had cleared).

In view of these observations, it is natural to ask 'What does it all mean?'. The following suggestions are tentative and have been raised because they fit in with other things that we know about dyslexics.

One very plausible theory is that it takes extra cognitive resources to *stop* yourself doing things, and dyslexics may have used up all their resources on the mathematical problem.

These behaviours were greatest in the younger dyslexics in my research but decreased with age. Perhaps this was a maturity factor where inhibitory processes develop with age. On the other hand, my father (a retired lecturer) wonders whether the dyslexics could have made these movements without thinking, to provide reassurance and a feeling of well-being in challenging circumstances. The chatter of these children leads me to think that these movements help in guiding the dyslexics through the problems. I have found subsequently in my own teaching that the technique of talking through a mathematical problem aloud is more effective than expecting them to work it out silently.

These responses reflect intense effort and the pressure that dyslexics put on themselves. It often happens that when we are confronted with some activity which we find challenging, we experience some level of anxiety. It is this anxiety or level of it that seems to hamper the dyslexic student more than the non-dyslexic. This can manifest itself as an inability to give the answer quickly or as having a 'mental block', which heightens the stress levels being experienced. It could be argued that the amount of stress increases with the level of difficulty and the effort required to be successful at the task. If the task were made more manageable and therefore more achievable, would the confidence level increase and the stress level decrease?

Matthew, my 8-year-old pupil, attempted to describe why he likes to move while working; he explained that when he fidgets, 'It makes my blood hot and it goes into my brain and makes me think.' Matthew is trying to tell us that the movements help to stimulate the brain when doing mathematics. Is this the dyslexic way of giving their all and in so doing, expending a larger amount of energy than seen in non-dyslexics?

The use of fingers to work out number facts seems vital for many dyslexics. In order to do calculations the dyslexics tend to use their fingers as a way of compensating for their weakness in memorising number facts; many dyslexics of all ages cannot count without some kind of concrete representation of the numbers that are being counted. Dyslexics particularly use their fingers when they are working on tables with obvious patterns, such as the $2\times$ and $5\times$ tables. Finger use may play a vital role in counting and arithmetical skill development and should not be discouraged.

There are a number of intriguing possible explanations for the characteristic behaviour of dyslexics. As educators we need to work alongside it and come to understand its role. It is possible that some of the available resources that the dyslexics have are spent on movement that then acts as a distraction, which works against the mathematical task in hand. However, if we ask the children to stop fidgeting we would be imposing on them yet another thing for them to think about and control, causing some sort of overload and a lessening of performance. This scenario presents a conflict of interests for the teacher and would be an interesting topic for systematic further research. In the meantime teachers should not rush to discourage such behaviour.

OVERALL CONCLUSIONS

Teaching suggestions

1   Suitable emphasis in teaching for the dyslexic might include:

   (a) Practice in writing numbers to dictation both fluently and accurately.
   (b) Naming large numbers such as 301,654, and counting numbers at speed, including counting across any mathematical barriers such as the ten barrier, both forwards and backwards.
   (c) Becoming adept at saying the number bonds to ten as swiftly as possible, for example, $7 + 3 = 10$.
   (d) Using the technique of doubling and halving numbers to work out a number fact.

2   As with literacy support, mathematical help can be enhanced by using multisensory strategies, as for example:

   (a) Using colour to highlight pattern in tables.
   (b) Employing as many of the senses as possible through 'doing', such as: counting on number lines, using finger techniques such as the 'gypsy' method of multiplication, and the 9 times table finger technique, using a multiplication grid to identify patterns, and developing interesting rhymes to help the dyslexic to remember the more difficult multiplication facts.
   (c) Developing a Mathematics Pack that is unique to each student. It is designed to review number facts and vocabulary, provide a means of remembering procedures for long division, also formulae, units, conversion factors, polygons and any other key points. It also provides rehearsal of the main algorithms. The Mathematics Pack evolves throughout the teaching programme and the learner is encouraged to take ownership of the Pack through participating in its construction and reviewing it regularly.
   (d) Presenting the knowledge in small manageable steps, each of which is successful.

3   Practical approaches to boosting confidence in the dyslexic learner might
    include:

    (a) Finding out how the dyslexic works out the mathematical problems
        and using this as a starting point. Showing interest in their approach.
    (b) Incorporating their interests into the lesson.
    (c) Concentrating on the easier number facts first.
    (d) Using mnemonics to tackle specific number facts.
    (e) Studying the relationships that the four operations share.
    (f) Avoiding fast talk that adds to confusion.
    (g) Helping the dyslexic appreciate that it is quite possible to be a good
        mathematician even if number facts are a challenge. Teachers should
        be careful to promote self-esteem in dyslexics – for this may be lost if
        they are slow at mathematical tasks and continually get them wrong.

4   Parents of dyslexic children can do much to provide mathematical support
    for their child. With greater awareness of the type of difficulties that their
    child might have, they can be guided to use appropriate strategies to
    rehearse number facts, perhaps more regularly than is possible at school.
    The Mathematics Pack is a good example of hands-on support which they
    can use.
5   Teachers should not try to suppress any additional behaviour exhibited by
    the learner that does not seem to contribute to answering the question. It
    may be necessary to work alongside this behaviour with a positive attitude.
6   If a mathematical task involving any of the four operations (multiplica-
    tion, division, addition and subtraction) is hard for a non-dyslexic, it is
    likely to be especially hard for a dyslexic.

REFERENCES

Henderson, A. and Miles, E. (2001) *Basic Topics in Mathematics for Dyslexics*, London,
    Whurr.
Jansons, K.M. (1988) 'A personal view of dyslexia and of thought without language',
    in L. Weiskrantz (ed.) *Thought Without Language*, Oxford, Oxford University
    Press.
MacMeeken, M. (1939) *Ocular Dominance in Relation to Developmental Aphasia*, London,
    University of London Press.
Rowling, J.K. (1997) *Harry Potter and the Philosopher's Stone*, London, Bloomsbury.
Steeves, K.J. (1983) 'Memory as a factor in the computational efficiency of dyslexic
    children with high abstract reasoning ability', *Annals of Dyslexia*, 33, 141–52.
Street, J. (1976) 'Sequencing and directional confusion in arithmetic', *Dyslexia Review*,
    15, 16–19.
Yeo, D. (2003) *Dyslexia, Dyspraxia and Mathematics*, London, Whurr.

Chapter 9

Children's arithmetical difficulties

Ann Dowker

There are many children and adults who experience difficulties with arithmetic (Ginsburg 1977; Basic Skills Agency 1997; Dowker 1998; Butterworth 1999). In this chapter, the term 'difficulties' simply refers to children or adults who struggle or fail to cope with some of the aspects of arithmetic which are necessary or desirable for educational or practical purposes. The use of the term does not mean that *all* such difficulties are pathological; that they are all classifiable as 'specific learning difficulties' in the technical sense, or that they must be either innate or the result of brain damage. Some difficulties with arithmetic may indeed involve a pathological process, as in the case of adults who lose previously established arithmetical concepts or skills as the result of brain damage. Most difficulties in arithmetic, like most difficulties in learned subjects, are likely to lie on a 'normal' continuum between extreme talent and extreme weakness; and are due not to brain damage but to a mismatch between an individual's pattern of cognitive strengths and weaknesses and the way that (s)he is taught.

However, there has recently been increased emphasis on the likelihood that, just as some children have dyslexia, some may have dyscalculia: a specific difficulty in doing arithmetic. The nature and frequency of such a problem has not yet been established. Some researchers have estimated that about 6 per cent of children might be diagnosed as dyscalculic. It is difficult, if not impossible, to establish a precise figure because arithmetical thinking involves such a wide variety of components; so that there are many forms and causes of arithmetical difficulty, which may assume different degrees of importance in different tasks and situations. If dyscalculia implies an impairment in *all* aspects of arithmetic, and *only* in arithmetic, then it would appear to be very rare (Dowker 1998): probably occurring in far fewer than 6 per cent of the population. If it implies difficulties with certain aspects of arithmetic, which are sufficient to cause significant practical and educational problems for the individual, then they are probably considerably more frequent than the 6 per cent figure would imply: perhaps occurring in 15–20 per cent of the population if not more. The exact figure is much less important than the fact that there are a large number of people who find arithmetic extremely difficult; fall increasingly behind in it during their school years; often come to fear it; and as adults are restricted by the need to avoid those jobs and other activities that involve arithmetic.

Jordan and Montani (1997) drew the distinction between developmental *delays* in arithmetic, where children simply take longer than others to acquire certain skills but eventually do acquire them, and developmental *deficits*, where there is a partial or total failure to acquire certain components of arithmetic. As with so many aspects of arithmetical development, it is difficult to tell to what extent the distinction between developmental deficits and delays reflects children's intrinsic characteristics, and to what extent it reflects environmental influences: perhaps in some cases a delay may be eventually overcome through appropriate teaching, while inappropriate teaching, or labelling the child as 'no good at maths', may lead to its remaining as a deficit.

This chapter will focus mainly on those characteristics *within* children that are associated with difficulties in arithmetic. It should be kept strongly in mind, however, that educational, cultural and other environmental factors have very strong influences on arithmetical performance. Indeed, the arithmetical performance of an individual represents such a strong and complex interaction between internal and environmental factors, that it is virtually impossible to separate the two types of influence, or to distinguish when internal factors end and environmental factors begin.

ARITHMETIC IS MADE UP OF MANY COMPONENTS

Arithmetical ability is sometimes treated as a single entity, but there is increasing evidence that it is made up of a number of components. There is no such thing as arithmetical ability: only arithmetical abilities. There are some aspects of arithmetic, such as counting and estimating small quantities, which seem to develop early and to be relatively easy for most people. There are other aspects, such as dealing with negative numbers and especially with fractions and decimals, which seem to create particular difficulty for many people. However, there is enormous individual variation, not only as regards overall performance in arithmetic, but also as regards relative strengths and weaknesses in the different aspects of arithmetic.

Studies of adult patients who have developed dyscalculia as a result of brain damage provide evidence that it is quite possible for one component of arithmetic to be selectively impaired, while others are preserved (Dehaene 1997; Butterworth 1999). For example, some patients can remember number facts such as multiplication tables, but no longer understand arithmetical principles such as the commutativity of addition and multiplication, while others understand the principles, but have serious trouble in remembering the facts (Warrington 1982; Delazer 2003). Some patients can estimate quantities, but cannot perform exact calculations, while others can calculate but not estimate (Dehaene 1997). Recently, functional brain imaging studies with healthy adults have given support to the view that different components of arithmetic may involve different areas or networks in the brain: for example, Dehaene and his colleagues found that exact calculation and estimation seem to involve rather different brain networks (Dehaene 1997).

Experimental and educational findings with typically developing children (Ginsburg 1977; Dowker 1998) and adults (Geary and Widaman 1992) have shown that it is possible for individuals to show marked discrepancies between almost any two possible components of arithmetic. For example, Dowker (1998) studied calculation and arithmetical reasoning in 213 unselected children between the ages of 6 and 9. She reported (p. 300) that '(1) individual differences in arithmetic are relatively marked; (2) that arithmetic is indeed not unitary and that it is relatively easy to find children with marked discrepancies between different components; and that (3) in particular it is risky to assume that a child "does not understand maths" because he or she performs poorly in some calculation tasks'. For example, she described individual children with discrepancies in both directions between arithmetical calculation and derived fact strategy use, and between arithmetical estimation and the estimation of quantities of objects.

Children with diagnosed arithmetical disabilities resemble both typical individuals and patients in frequently showing strong discrepancies between different components. For example, some are particularly impaired in remembering number facts; some in remembering how to carry out procedures; and some in understanding the principles of arithmetic (Temple 1991; Geary 1993; Macaruso and Sokol 1998; Jordan and Hanich 2000).

HOW SPECIFIC ARE DIFFICULTIES IN ARITHMETIC?

The question arises as to whether developmental difficulties in arithmetic are typically specific to arithmetic, or whether they are usually caused by deficits in abilities that affect other abilities besides arithmetic.

Butterworth (1999) has proposed that there is a 'number module' in the brain, which is responsible for very basic numerical skills, such as recognition of sets of up to 3 items without counting them. This may be based predominantly in the left parietal lobe. If the number module fails to develop, then this will result in dyscalculia. Alternatively (or in an additional group of individuals), arithmetical difficulties may result from impairments that are not specific to arithmetic, but do affect at least some aspects of arithmetic.

In fact, at least within the brain, the distinction between areas specifically related to arithmetic and those which are involved in other functions that facilitate arithmetic may not be completely clear-cut. Many brain imaging studies suggest that arithmetic and even its more delimited subcomponents are represented in the brain by networks rather than by single localized areas, and such networks may include areas related to numerous different functions. Relevant functions may, for example, include motor skills; verbal abilities; spatial abilities; and/or memory.

Motor co-ordination

Before considering the cognitive functions that might be associated with arithmetic, we should first consider the potential effects of difficulties in motor co-ordination: especially in the motor skills involved in using the fingers for counting. There is some evidence that difficulties with the motor skills involved in counting may impair the acquisition of counting and arithmetic (Camos et al. 1998). However, they certainly do not always do so. Children with serious difficulties in the physical procedure of counting can still be very able at arithmetical calculation and reasoning.

For example, one of the children included in Dowker's (1998) study was Daniel, who had cerebral palsy which prevented him from controlling his hands sufficiently well to co-ordinate pointing to objects with verbal counting. At the age of 7, he could not count 10 objects reliably. Yet he obtained a scaled score of 14 (well above average) on the WISC Arithmetic subtest, and performed better than most of his classmates on calculation and derived fact strategy tasks.

More studies of children with motor difficulties affecting counting would be desirable. Different aspects of counting difficulty need to be separated: for example, differences between counting fingers and counting other objects; and between motor difficulties in performing the act of counting, and perceptual difficulties in seeing and interpreting the result.

Language and arithmetic: could language difficulties cause arithmetical difficulties?

There is little doubt that arithmetical difficulties can be associated with language difficulties. It appears that unusual patterns of brain function are associated with language difficulties, but the extent and nature of the association are still unclear. Following current practice, the term 'specific language impairment' will here be used to refer to marked delays or abnormalities in the production or comprehension of spoken language that cannot be explained by low nonverbal IQ, hearing impairment, emotional problems, or environmental deprivation. 'Dyslexia' will be used to refer to difficulties in reading or writing which are similarly unexplainable by other factors, though many contemporary definitions of dyslexia involve far more stringent criteria for its manifestations, both with regard to literacy and other characteristics (e.g. Nicolson and Fawcett 1995).

Arithmetical difficulties may be associated with spoken and written language impairments (Fazio 1994, 1996; Donlan 1998, 2003). Children with specific language impairment and, to a lesser extent, dyslexia, often have difficulty with those aspects of arithmetic that involve verbal memory. They may be very delayed in learning the sequence of numbers in counting; and later on, in learning number facts. Word problem-solving is also likely to be particularly weak in such children. In fact, word problems represent a source of difficulty for many children, and success with them appears to be influenced by variations in verbal ability well within the normal range: one does not need to have a language impairment to become confused by the language of word problems.

Serious difficulties with early arithmetic are often associated with difficulties in understanding mathematics-related terms such as 'more than' and 'less than' (Sue Tomkys, personal communication). Such problems are often, though not always, linked to more general language difficulties.

Most arithmetical difficulties associated with dyslexia tend to involve problems restricted to such verbal aspects of arithmetic, rather than difficulties with arithmetical concepts. However, Yeo (2003) reports that a small but significant number of dyslexic children do have difficulties with 'number sense': they comprehend numbers solely in terms of quantities to be counted and do not understand them in more abstract ways, or perceive the relationships between different numbers. Yeo suggests that the counting sequence presents so much difficulty for this group that it absorbs their attention and prevents them from considering other aspects of number. This sort of difficulty occurs in some children who are not dyslexic (Gray 1997); and at present the extent to which it is particularly associated with dyslexia is not yet established. The existence, but relatively small size, of such a group among dyslexic children may in part explain the conflicting findings about the relationship of conceptual problems with arithmetic to verbal versus spatial disabilities.

Studies of adults with acquired language impairment (aphasia) following damage to the left hemisphere of the brain have suggested that arithmetic is often but not always impaired, and that some aspects of arithmetic are more likely to be impaired than others. For example, Delazer *et al.* (1999) found that aphasic patients were particularly impaired in the retrieval of multiplication facts. They suggested that verbal processing is particularly important in the memory for multiplication tables. Dyslexic children also often show particular difficulty with multiplication tables (Miles 1993).

However, many people with arithmetical difficulties have no problems with language; and there are some arithmetical 'savants' who perform certain arithmetical tasks at an impressive level despite having very limited language abilities (Hermelin and O'Connor 1990; Heavey 2003).

Spatial abilities

There are frequent suggestions that spatial abilities are important in arithmetic; though the exact nature of their contribution to arithmetic – as opposed to certain other components of arithmetic such as geometry – is not always made clear. Some degree of spatial ability is necessary for the correct placement and alignment of digits, and as such must play a part in multi-digit arithmetic, especially written arithmetic. Inversions, misplacements and misalignments of digits occur in what is sometimes referred to as 'spatial dyscalculia' (Hartje 1987). Moreover, there are suggestions that mental arithmetic, and the ordering of numbers, can be represented by spatial positions on an imaginary number line. 8 may be seen as higher than 7 on a vertical number line, or to the right of 7 on a horizontal number line. Subtracting 5 may be represented internally as moving down or back five places on such a number line. It is also possible that spatial representations of the mathematical relationships in a word problem can facilitate its solution.

Such theories about the role of spatial ability in mental arithmetic are still, however, controversial. First of all, there is much evidence for individual differences in the ways in which number and arithmetic are represented. Some individuals make very strong use of internal number lines and other spatial representations (Seron *et al.* 1994); some people make much less use of such representations. It would be interesting to investigate the extent to which individual differences in mode of representation are associated with individual differences in arithmetical performance. The evidence so far suggests that there may be little or no such association: people of similar arithmetical ability may represent numbers and arithmetical operations in quite different ways. Studies of mathematicians have suggested that some of them represent numerical problems in a mainly spatial way; some in a mainly verbal way; and some in an abstract way that cannot be properly defined as either.

Some genetic disorders such as Williams syndrome, Turner syndrome and the chromosome 22q11.2 deletion syndrome are associated with both arithmetical and spatial difficulties. However, many children with arithmetical difficulties have no obvious spatial difficulties.

Rourke (1993) has proposed that there are two main subtypes of arithmetic disabilities, the first associated with right hemisphere dysfunction and the second with left hemisphere dysfunction. In the first, reading is unimpaired; verbal IQ is superior to nonverbal IQ, and there may even be 'nonverbal learning disabilities' involving spatial and social learning deficits, and indications of right hemisphere dysfunction; and the arithmetical disabilities involve predominantly conceptual deficits. In the second, reading is also impaired; nonverbal IQ is superior to verbal IQ; and the arithmetical disabilities are mostly memory-related. However, others, such as Shalev (1997), found no such distinction. Indeed, Jordan and her colleagues (Jordan and Montani 1997; Jordan and Hanich 2000; Jordan *et al.* 2003) found what seems to be the opposite, though they did not directly investigate verbal/nonverbal IQ discrepancies. In their studies, children with specific arithmetical disabilities tended to have problems mostly with memory for facts, while those with combined reading/arithmetic disabilities had problems with arithmetical reasoning and problem-solving.

Dowker (1995, 1998) found that children who are much better at derived fact strategy use than calculation often show marked discrepancies between WISC Performance and Verbal IQ scores. These discrepancies are equally likely to be in either direction: it is the existence of such a discrepancy, not its direction, that seems to be associated with a superiority of derived fact strategy use over calculation.

Memory difficulties

The types of memory most commonly investigated with regard to arithmetical difficulties are long-term memory for facts and 'working memory': the ability to keep track of information, and to use it to guide ones actions.

Memory for facts

There is no doubt that memory for arithmetical facts is a very common source of difficulty for people who perform poorly in arithmetic. There are people who have difficulties with arithmetic, despite a good memory for number facts; but, on the whole, poor memory for number facts is one of the problems most commonly found in people with diagnosed difficulties in arithmetic (Russell and Ginsburg 1984; Ostad 1998).

One should not leap to the conclusion that poor memory for number facts is *causing* the arithmetical difficulties. First, one reason for such findings may be that memory for number facts features prominently in many of the tests that are used to diagnose difficulties in arithmetic: thus, people who fail to remember number facts may be more likely to have their arithmetical difficulties *diagnosed* than those with other kinds of problem. For another thing, if people find it difficult to understand or perform arithmetic for other reasons, then this may make the facts harder to remember. Nonetheless, some people do seem to have a specific difficulty with number facts, without having the difficulty with other aspects of arithmetic. This has been found both for children (Ginsburg 1977; Dowker 1995, 1998); for healthy adults with calculation difficulties (Dowker 1994); and for some adult patients following brain damage (Warrington 1982).

Children and adults who have difficulty in remembering arithmetical facts may compensate by using alternative strategies. These include counting strategies; derived fact strategies that involve arithmetical principles such as commutativity, and combinations of the two. For example, Miles (1993) describes dyslexic pupils who were able to work out suitable strategies for solving mathematical reasoning problems from the Superior Adult level of the Terman-Merrill IQ test, but had difficulty with the relatively simple calculations involved. For example, one 16-year-old boy was given the 'tree' item, which involves telling the individual the heights of a tree at planting and at yearly intervals over the next three years. (S)he is then required to work out its height at the end of the fourth year, which involves finding a pattern in its growth over the successive years. He worked out the pattern correctly, but miscalculated $27 - 18$ as 11.

Many if not most dyslexic individuals show poor short-term and long-term memory for number facts, while being unimpaired at dealing with arithmetical concepts and principles (Steeves 1983; Miles 1993; Turner-Ellis 2002). However, there are also many non-dyslexic individuals who show very similar discrepancies between the factual and conceptual aspects of arithmetic. Claire, one of the adults studies by Dowker (1994), showed no signs of dyslexia and had a gift for learning foreign languages, but had difficulty in memorizing arithmetical facts and at the age of 10 made a very similar type of response to the Terman-Merrill 'tree' problem, working out the pattern correctly and devising a correct strategy, but adding $27+13$ as 39.

It is still unclear whether such difficulties with memory for facts are typically specific to numbers, or whether they are usually the result of more general difficulties with memory for facts.

Working memory, planning and control

One important aspect of arithmetic is the ability to carry out arithmetical procedures flexibly and accurately; to remember, monitor, and reflect on these procedures; and to keep track of the steps and partial results within these procedures. This ability is dependent, at least in part, on 'working memory', which includes the ability to actively rehearse and keep track of information in short-term memory, and to use both short-term and long-term memory to guide one's actions.

There is evidence that difficulties in working memory are related to difficulties in arithmetic (Hitch and McCauley 1991; Adams and Hitch 1998). For example, children who can hold very few sums or numbers in memory at the same time tend to be less good at arithmetic than those who can hold many sums or numbers in memory at the same time. Arithmetical ability is more closely associated with working memory for numbers than for other types of material such as words. It is still unclear to what extent working memory difficulties *cause* problems with arithmetic and to what extent it is the difficulties with arithmetic that cause problems with working memory for numbers.

Severe specific difficulties with arithmetic

There are some individuals who have very severe difficulties with most aspects of arithmetic, while having no apparent difficulties in other areas. Butterworth (1999) described 'Charles', a university graduate, who had no problems with literacy or general reasoning, but who could solve even single-digit sums only by counting slowly on his fingers. He could not subtract or divide at all, or carry out any sort of multi-digit arithmetic. He was extremely slow even at comparing numbers: for example, saying which was bigger, 9 or 3. He could only give the answer to such comparison problems after counting on his fingers from the smaller number to the larger number. He took about ten times as long as most people even to state whether two numerals were the same or different. He seemed to lack even the most basic numerical abilities that usually seem to be present in babies: he could not even recognize two dots as two without counting them.

Such extreme cases are rare, even among those with diagnosed dyscalculia. Nicola, for example, is a 20-year-old woman who has been diagnosed as having dyscalculia. She has always had severe difficulties with school arithmetic. Her WAIS Arithmetic subtest score is 2. On the British Abilities Scales Basic Number Skills subtest, designed for children, she obtained an age equivalent score of 8 years 9 months. This test places considerable emphasis on the ability to read 2- and 3-digit numbers, which Nicola can do. It is possible that a test which place less emphasis on number reading would have resulted in an even lower age equivalent. She deals with most arithmetical problems by counting on her fingers: counting on from the larger number for addition; counting down from the larger number for subtraction. What are her more basic numerical difficulties like? Her ability to estimate numerosities is indeed relatively weak; but she *can* recognize quantities up to 3 without difficulty. There is a sharp division for her between 3 and more than 3: for larger quantities she counts on from 3, so that 6 dots are counted: '3, 4, 5, 6'.

It is important that people like Charles, and even like Nicola, be identified early on as having difficulties, so as to reduce the risks of intellectual confusion and emotional frustration and possibly humiliation if they are expected to cope with the typical school arithmetic curriculum without special help.

CONCLUSIONS

Difficulties with arithmetic are common. Severe arithmetical difficulties are usually not completely domain-specific, but tend to be associated with other difficulties; for example, with motor skills, language, spatial skills, and/or memory (though there is still uncertainty as to the extent to which memory difficulties can be specific to the domain of arithmetic).

However, some people do have severe specific difficulties with arithmetic; and more have mild specific difficulties with arithmetic.

It is as yet unclear whether the specificity or otherwise of an individual's arithmetical difficulties actually influences the nature of such difficulties, or the appropriate interventions for ameliorating such difficulties. What is perhaps more crucial is the fact that arithmetical difficulties usually affect only some, and not all, components of arithmetic. It is important that, as far as possible, interventions for individuals with arithmetical difficulties should be adapted to the specific patterns of strengths and weaknesses shown by the individuals concerned (Weaver 1954; Wright *et al.* 2000; Dowker 2001).

ACKNOWLEDGEMENTS

I am grateful to the ESRC and the Esmee Fairbairn Charitable Trust for financial support. I would like to thank the teachers and children in the Oxford primary schools where I have worked, for all their help and co-operation. I am grateful to the members of the Numeracy Intervention e-mail discussion group for their interesting and helpful comments on related issues.

REFERENCES

Adams, J. and Hitch, G. (1998) 'Children's mental arithmetic and working memory', in C. Donlan (ed.) *The Development of Mathematical Skills*, Hove, Psychology Press, pp. 153–73.

Basic Skills Agency (1997) *International Numeracy Survey: A Comparison of the Basic Numeracy Skills of Adults 16 to 60 in Seven Countries*, London, Basic Skills Agency.

Butterworth, B. (1999) *The Mathematical Brain*, London, Macmillan.

Camos, V., Fayol, M., Lacert, P., Bardi, A. and Lacquiere, C. (1998) 'Counting in dysphasic and dyspraxic children', *A.N.A.E.*, 10, 86–91.

Dehaene, S. (1997) *The Number Sense*, London, Macmillan.

Delazer, M. (2003) 'Neuropsychological findings on conceptual knowledge of arithmetic', in A. Baroody and A. Dowker (eds) *The Development of Arithmetical Concepts and Skills*, Mahwah, NJ, Erlbaum, pp. 385–407.

Delazer, M., Girelli, L., Semenza, C. and Denes, G. (1999) 'Numerical skills and aphasia', *Journal of the International Neuropsychological Society*, 5, 213–21.

Donlan, C. (1998) 'Number without language? Studies of children with specific language impairments', in C. Donlan (ed.) *The Development of Mathematical Skills*, Hove, Psychology Press, pp. 255–74.

Donlan, C. (2003) 'Early numeracy skills in children with specific language impairment: number system knowledge and arithmetical strategies', in A. Baroody and A. Dowker (eds) *The Development of Arithmetical Concepts and Skills*, Mahwah, NJ, Erlbaum, pp. 337–58.

Dowker, A.D. (1994) 'Adults with mild specific calculation difficulties', Paper delivered at British Psychological Society London Conference, 19 December 1994.

Dowker, A.D. (1995) 'Children with specific calculation difficulties', *Links2*, 2, 7–12.

Dowker, A.D. (1998) 'Individual differences in normal arithmetical development', in C. Donlan (ed.) *The Development of Mathematical Skills*, Hove, Psychology Press, pp. 275–302.

Dowker, A.D. (2001) 'Numeracy recovery: a pilot scheme for early intervention with young children with numeracy difficulties', *Support for Learning*, 16, 6–10.

Fazio, B. (1994) 'The counting abilities of children with specific language impairments: a comparison of oral and gestural tasks', *Journal of Speech and Hearing Research*, 37, 358–68.

Fazio, B. (1996) 'Mathematical abilities of children with specific language impairments: a follow-up study', *Journal of Speech and Hearing Research*, 39, 839–49.

Geary, D.C. (1993) 'Mathematical disabilities: cognitive, neuropsychological and genetic components', *Psychological Bulletin*, 114, 345–62.

Geary, D.C. and Widaman, K.F. (1992) 'Numerical cognition: on the convergence of componential and psychometric models', *Intelligence*, 16, 47–80.

Ginsburg, H.P. (1977) *Children's Arithmetic*, New York, Teachers' College Press.

Gray, E. (1997) 'Compressing the counting process: developing a flexible interpretation of symbols', in I. Thompson (ed.) *Teaching and Learning Early Number*, London, Open University Press.

Hartje, W. (1987) 'The effect of spatial disorders on arithmetical skills', in G. Deloche and X. Seron (eds) *Mathematical Disabilities: A Cognitive Neuropsychological Perspective*, Hillsdale, NJ, Erlbaum, pp. 121–36.

Heavey, L. (2003) 'Arithmetical savants', in A. Baroody and A. Dowker (eds) *The Development of Arithmetical Concepts and Skills*, Mahwah, NJ, Erlbaum, pp. 409–34.

Hermelin, B. and O'Connor, N. (1990) 'Factors and primes: a specific numerical ability', *Psychological Medicine*, 20, 163–9.

Hitch, G. and McCauley, E. (1991) 'Working memory in children with specific arithmetical learning difficulties', *British Journal of Psychology*, 82, 375–86.

Jordan, N.C. and Hanich, L.B. (2000) 'Mathematical thinking in second grade children with different forms of LD', *Journal of Learning Disabilities*, 33, 567–78.

Jordan, N.C. and Montani, T.O. (1997) 'Cognitive arithmetic and problem solving: a comparison of children with specific and general mathematics difficulties', *Journal of Learning Disabilities*, 30, 624–34.

Jordan, N.C., Hanich, L. and Uberti, H.Z. (2003) 'Mathematical thinking and learning difficulties', in A. Baroody and A. Dowker (eds) *The Development of Arithmetical Concepts and Skills*, Mahwah, NJ, Erlbaum, pp. 359–84.

Macaruso, P. and Sokol, S.M. (1998) 'Cognitive neuropsychology and developmental dyscalculia', in C. Donlan (ed.) *The Development of Mathematical Skills*, Hove, Psychology Press, pp. 201–25.

Miles, T.R. (1993) *Dyslexia: The Pattern of Difficulties* (2nd edn), London, Whurr.

Nicolson, R.I. and Fawcett, A.J. (1995) 'Dyslexia is more than a phonological disability', *Dyslexia: An International Journal of Research and Practice*, 1(1), 19–36.

Ostad, S. (1998) 'Developmental differences in solving simple arithmetic word problems and simple number fact problems: a comparison of mathematically normal and mathematically disabled children', *Mathematical Cognition*, 4, 1–20.

Rourke, B.P. (1993) 'Arithmetical disabilities specific and otherwise: a neuropsychological perspective', *Journal of Learning Disabilities*, 26, 214–26.

Russell, R.L. and Ginsburg, H.P. (1984) 'Cognitive analysis of children's mathematical difficulties', *Cognition and Instruction*, 1, 217–44.

Seron, X., Pesenti. M., Noel, M., Deloche, G. and Cornet, J.A. (1994) 'Images of numbers, or when 98 is upper left and 6 sky blue', *Cognition*, 44, 159–96.

Shalev, R.S. (1997) 'Neuropsychological aspects of developmental dyscalculia', *Mathematical Cognition*, 3, 105–20.

Steeves, K.J. (1983) 'Memory as a factor in the computational efficiency of dyslexic children with high abstract reasoning ability', *Annals of Dyslexia*, 33, 141–52.

Temple, C.M. (1991) 'Procedural dyscalculia and number fact dyscalculia: double dissociation in developmental dyscalculia', *Cognitive Neuropsychology*, 8, 155–76.

Turner-Ellis, S.A. (2002) 'Correctness and speed of dyslexics and non-dyslexics in the four mathematical operations', University of Liverpool, Unpublished PhD thesis.

Warrington, E.K. (1982) 'The fractionation of arithmetical skills: a single case study', *Quarterly Journal of Experimental Psychology*, 34A, 31–51.

Weaver, F.J. (1954) 'Differentiated instruction in arithmetic: an overview and a promising trend', *Education*, 74, 300–5.

Wright, R.J., Martland, J. and Stafford, A. (2000) *Early Numeracy: Assessment for Teaching and Intervention*, London, Paul Chapman.

Yeo, D. (2003) *Dyslexia, Dyspraxia and Mathematics*, London, Whurr.

Chapter 10

An overview

Elaine Miles

The contributions in this book have been written independently, and from an individual point of view. It may be useful, therefore, to look at what information they give us overall on the balances of strengths and weaknesses that dyslexics are likely to have in mathematics and the approaches which have the best potential for helping them. It seems that the main difficulties are in the area of number work, rather than in spatial areas, for example, geometry.

In the first chapter, T.R. Miles has cited a number of teaching observations and research studies which throw light on these matters. He mentions the following:

1 left–right confusion – an important factor, in that for some calculations it is traditional practice to start on the left, and for others on the right. (Yeo 2003 is inclined to encourage methods which consistently start on the left.)
2 The necessity for dyslexics often to use compensatory concrete strategies such as making marks on paper or using their fingers, because they cannot remember number facts or complicated algorithms. (They retreat to the simple algorithm that numbers go up in ones.)
3 The fact that they 'lose track' in reciting multiplication tables, and get in a muddle over carrying figures (so may prefer to start on the left always). A very devastating result of short-term memory problems is the inability of dyslexics to remember number facts.

Miles illustrates the imbalance of skills with reports of performances on the mathematics test in the large-scale British Births Cohort Study of 1970 (Miles *et al.* 2001). Those who satisfied the criteria for dyslexia had distinctive difficulties on some questions compared with the other children.

Miles also discusses other developmental anomalies that are now the subject of research, and their relations with dyslexia. As regards *dyspraxia* he quotes Yeo's recent work. She found that poorly co-ordinated children (dyspraxics) had many of the same number problems as dyslexics, and that similar methods helped them; some of them, however, had no short-term memory problems, whereas only some dyslexics, not all, had poor co-ordination problems. These are the things to keep in mind in teaching. Yeo decided that the best way of helping them was to provide a single method for each type of calculation that was most congenial to them, and she calls these 'big value methods'. With regard to *ADHD*, Miles finds the use of this term still somewhat controversial, and its relevance to attention and concentration not yet clarified. As for *dyscalculia*, he refers to the DfES Numeracy Strategy Guidance Leaflet, which suggests that the majority of those with particular difficulties in mathematics also have the language difficulties associated with dyslexia. Miles says that it is still an open question as to whether it is more useful to treat dyslexia and dyscalculia as separate syndromes. He describes cases he has met of individuals who had arithmetical problems without literacy problems, who nevertheless seemed to show some of the other commonly observed weaknesses of dyslexics. He also points to some of the incidental features of Butterworth's (2003) screening test which, quite apart from any question of dyscalculia, would present problems for dyslexics. Finally he quotes the remarkably similar prevalence figures in two studies of dyscalculia in India, conducted by two different researchers, Ramaa and Gowramma at an interval of ten years.

Steve Chinn has updated his chapter on individual diagnosis and cognitive style with the latest information on methods of testing, and new work on errors, where he found that *in timed conditions*, dyslexics' errors did not differ quantitatively from those of non-dyslexics, but they were more likely not to attempt questions on which they might fail. There is probably nowhere in this country where more knowledge about the testing and teaching of mathematics to dyslexics of secondary age is to be found than at Mark College; this is through the dedicated work of Chinn and his colleague Richard Ashcroft, from whom a second contribution comes later in this book. Chinn has more to say, also, on the importance of taking note of differences in cognitive style among individuals, whether dyslexic or non-dyslexic, and has some new and interesting observations on the relevance of this in framing curricula, which need to have some flexibility and not enforce a particular style.

The next four chapters are not substantially changed from the previous edition. Mary Kibel's imaginative description of how she solved basic difficulties of younger children with the 'four rules' makes the important point that this needs to involve not only practical action, but also oral contribution from the child as it does these manoeuvres. Vygotsky (1986) would no doubt say that the child's words describing the methods he is using get internalised in this way and become his thoughts. This lesson is an important one also for those teachers who teach literacy skills to even slightly older dyslexics; we need to get the pupils to speak, not just hand out instructions to them! Another truth that emerges from Kibel's chapter is, of course, how much can be achieved by a teacher who is as imaginative as her. Pupils have imaginations which can be harnessed, and enjoyment is important. I once witnessed a specialist teacher in training say goodbye to her pupil with the words 'Go away and *practise* your reading.' Oh dear – memories of learning scales! There are some things which need to be 'practised', for example, the spelling pack, but reading is to be enjoyed.

Elaine Miles reminds us how complex are the ways in which reading is involved in mathematics, and all these may be an obstacle for the dyslexic. It is obvious, of course that the level of difficulty in the wording of a question may be too high, but also the word order is different from that in a story book, condensed, sometimes tortuous, and the order of the information one wants in solving the problem is not always the same as that presented in the question. Next there is the problem of the use of everyday vocabulary in a quite other, technical, sense, and the addition of abstruse technical vocabulary whose meaning is not at all obvious from previous words one knows. Mathematics has also a complicated symbolic language of its own, different for each topic, it seems, and sometimes conflicting with written language usage (for instance in algebra letters of the alphabet have nothing to do with phonology, and 'Horrors!' there are Greek letters too in some mathematical areas.) Finally place value has a language of its own, and the use of different brackets for different purposes is also complicated.

In discussing difficulties at the secondary stage, Anne Henderson is looking at them from a different angle from that of Steve Chinn (although he has already mentioned the reluctance of the dyslexic pupil to risk failure by attempting a question that he is not confident about). Anne is concerned with boosting the pupil's self-confidence, and with creating a relationship between teacher and pupil in which he can learn. Part of this involves studying carefully where he/she has gone wrong. He may understand the concepts perfectly well, but just be making some little mistake, for example, by pressing the wrong button on the calculator. Calculators have their traps for the unwary too. The pupil should not be given an impression of utter failure; the teacher must highlight his successes to encourage him. A show of impatience by the teacher will not help – teacher and pupil need to work as partners. Anne mentions aids which can be introduced. The teacher has to make the lesson interesting, and show that she believes in her pupil.

T.R. Miles describes how the use of materials such as Dienes' blocks, similar to those used by Mary Kibel, can be helpful even with older pupils. The materials used need not be childish – one obviously would not choose the coloured Cuisenaire rods, but some of the more modern Base Ten materials produced are neither heavy nor clumsy, and are invaluable as a basis for adult-level discussion about the number system and about symbols and symbolisation (including the symbol '0'). The blocks can also be used to make clear what 'decomposition' involves, and what 'indices' represent, and can even be used to demonstrate the binomial theorem! (Students may also be interested to discuss the value of alternative ways of representing the number system – there is the Roman notation, for instance. However, the Arabic system which we use is much more adaptable to very large numbers and to the very small ones needed in some branches of science.)

Steve Chinn and Richard Ashcroft outline their principles in teaching mathematics to dyslexics. They observe that these have difficulty in mastering interrelationships and developing generalisations, but think that methods of teaching them should not compromise the structure and unitary character of mathematics. Strategies which develop a sound understanding of the subject will be more effective long-term, they say, in improving the weak areas, than rote learning, even with, mnemonics or music. The use of patterns, however, is logical and serves their basic objective. Two collections of facts, from 0 to 9, and number bonds to 10, are, however essential, and one concept, that of place value. Having made these minimum requirements clear, they next steer us through the patterns in the numbers 1–100. This approach will unify all aspects of numeracy, rather than treating addition, subtraction, multiplication and division as separate subjects. This is challenging.

Sula Turner Ellis focuses on a particular major problem for dyslexics – the acquisition of number facts, on which she has herself done some research, and is using the results to steer her in her teaching. In the group that she studied – children aged 7–15 years – she has pinpointed the age at which pupils can most easily make progress in accuracy and speed in this area as between ten-and-a-half and twelve-and a-half year. Review is then needed to avoid a likely decline in the teenage years. Of course to start teaching these facts even earlier may very likely be more valuable still, as with all teaching of dyslexics, but this still needs investigation.

Crossing the ten barriers in calculations is a particular obstacle which has to be overcome by practice at all points, with flash cards representing number bonds that cross the barriers (for twenties and thirties as well as for ten itself). The principle, along with its representation on paper by place value, can be imaginatively portrayed, for example, by a tree (as unit), a wood (for the tens), and a forest (for the hundreds). However, there are 'barriers' in many areas – between whole numbers and decimals and within decimals, in the money system etc. In addition dyslexics are slow, so need a lot of practice to become fluent. Sula has observed that dyslexics fidget a lot – exaggerated tongue and lip movements, movements of the head, facial grimaces, making comments, etc. She thinks it is unhelpful to try to stop them. Perhaps they need the activity as reassurance under stress; talking them through a problem may give them some outlet. Sula's concluding section sums up her suggestions for teachers.

Ann Dowker gives an altogether new perspective, which is very refreshing. She writes about children's arithmetical difficulties in general, rather than those of dyslexics in particular, basing her information on her study of unselected children between 6 and 9 years of age in Oxfordshire schools – which led to a chapter she contributed to a book on the development of mathematical skills (Dowker 1998). (She reminds us that educational, cultural and other environmental factors are very influential, and it is almost impossible to separate these from the constitutional factors, because of the complex interaction.)

However, she says, there is enormous individual variation, not only in overall performance, but in the relative strengths and weaknesses in different aspects of arithmetic, even between arithmetical estimation and estimation of quantities of objects, between calculation and derived fact strategy. Children with diagnosed arithmetical disabilities show similar strong discrepancies. Moreover, the distinction between areas specifically related to arithmetic and those involved in other cognitive functions does not seem to be clear-cut. Unlike Butterworth (1999), who posited a 'number module' based predominately in the left parietal lobe, Dowker argues that brain imaging suggests that arithmetic, and even its sub-components, are represented by networks rather than single localised areas. She then describes how different skills and abilities may affect arithmetic – motor co-ordination, language skills, spatial abilities, memory (long-term and 'working memory'), planning and control abilities. Although there do exist cases of individuals who have severe difficulties with most aspects of arithmetic but seem to have no other problems, these are extremely rare. More usually arithmetical difficulties affect some components but not all, and are related to difficulties in other areas of function as well.

There is a very varied assortment of contributions in this book, but taken together they offer the fruits of much practical experience and a wide range of insights for the teacher of dyslexics whose pupils have arithmetical difficulties as well as literacy ones.

REFERENCES

Butterworth, B. (1999) *The Mathematical Brain*, London, Macmillan.

Butterworth, B. (2003) *Dyscalculia Screener*, Windsor, NFER-NELSON.

Dowker, A.D. (1998) 'Individual differences in normal arithmetical development', in C. Donlan (ed.) *The Development of Mathematical Thinking*, Psychology Press.

Miles, T.R., Haslum, M.N. and Wheeler, T.J. (2001) 'Mathematical difficulties of 10-year-old dyslexic children', *Annals of Dyslexia*, L1, 299–331.

Ramaa, S. and Gowramma, I.P. (2002) 'A systematic procedure for identifying dyslexic children in India', *Dyslexia: An International Journal of Research and Practice*, 8(2), 67–85.

Vygotsky, L. (1986) *'Thought and Language'* (translated by A. Kozulin), Cambridge, MA, MIT Press.

Yeo, D. (2003) *Dyslexia, Dyspraxia and Mathematics*, London, Whurr.

Appendix

Proof of gypsy multiplication

Let x and y be any numbers between 1 and 5.

The fingers on one hand will therefore be $5 + x$ and the fingers on the other hand $5 + y$.

It is required to prove that

$$(5 + x)(5 + y) = 10(x + y) + (5 - x)(5 - y)$$

Now $(5 + x)(5 + y) = 25 + 5x + 5y + xy$, while

$$10(x + y) = 10x + 10y \quad \text{and} \quad (5 - x)(5 - y) = 25 - 5x - 5y + xy$$

So $10(x + y) + (5 - x)(5 - y) = 10x + 10y + 25 - 5x - 5y + xy$.

If we then add $5x + 5y$ to both sides we are left with $5x + 5y + 25 + xy = (5 + x)(5 + y)$. $\hfill$ QED.

Suggested reading

Chinn, S.J. (1996) *What to do When You Can't Learn Times Tables*, Baldock, Egon.

Chinn, S.J. (1999) *What to do When You Can't do Addition and Subtraction*, Baldock, Egon.

Chinn, S.J. (2004) *The Trouble with Maths: A Practical Guide to Helping Learners with Numeracy Difficulties*, London: RoutledgeFalmer.

Chinn, S.J. and Ashcroft, R. (1998) *Mathematics for Dyslexics* (2nd edn), London, Whurr.

DfES (2001) *The National Numeracy Strategy and Guidance to Support Pupils with Dyslexia and Dyscalculia*, DfES 2051 212001.

Durkin, K. and Shire, B. (1991) *Language in Mathematical Education: Research and Practice*, Milton Keynes, Open University Press.

Henderson, A. (1998) *Maths for the Dyslexic: A Practical Guide*, London, David Fulton.

Hendersøn, A. and Miles, E. (2001) *Basic Topics in Mathematics for Dyslexics*, London, Whurr.

The Numeracy Strategy. Framework for Teaching Mathematics from Reception to Year 6 (1999) London, Department for Education and Employment.

Yeo, D. (2003) *Dyslexia, Dyspraxia and Mathematics*, London, Whurr.

Walton, Margaret (1994) *Maths Words*. Obtained from Margaret Walton, 17, Bryn Bras, Llanfairpwll, Anglesey, LL61 5PX.

Name index

Subject index

---

1 References to arithmetic and the four arithmetical operations, multiplication, division, addition and subtraction, occur throughout the book and have therefore not been indexed.